FRESH-WATER FISHES

Text by
JURAJ HOLČÍK AND JOZEF MIHÁLIK

Illustrations by
JIŘÍ MALÝ

SPRING BOOKS

Translated by S. Kadečka

Designed and produced by
ARTIA for SPRING BOOKS

Published by
The Hamlyn Publishing Group Limited
London • New York • Sydney • Toronto
Hamlyn House, Feltham, Middlesex, England

© 1968 Paul Hamlyn Ltd and Artia
First edition 1968
Second impression 1969
Third impression 1970
Fourth impression 1972
ISBN 0 600 01294 8

Printed in Czechoslovakia by Svoboda, Prague
S 2727

Introduction

Fishes belong to the subphylum Craniata, which contains all the animals with a skull, or cranium, and a segmented backbone. They are also cold-blooded, more accurately described as 'poikilothermic' which means that their body temperature changes with the external temperature.

The twelve classes of fishes differ from each other in many respects, but are generally similar in their aquatic habitat which in turn imposes limitations on shape, so that they are also similar in their streamlined form. Five of the named classes are extinct and known only from fossil remains.

This book contains selected examples of the most highly developed group, the Teleosts, fishes with a bony skeleton. It is estimated that there are over 15,000 species of Teleosts, in freshwater and salt water, making this the most numerous group among the vertebrates.

The body of a fish consists of head, trunk and tail. It is usually streamlined so that there is no distinct demarcation between the three regions. The division between head and trunk is marked by the gill slits, and between trunk and tail the anus provides a convenient indication of where the body cavity ends.

Typically, a fish has two sets of paired fins and three median fins. The paired fins are the pectorals — attached to the pectoral girdle and comparable with the 'arms' of higher vertebrates — and the pelvic or ventral fins — comparable with 'legs'. These fins are used mainly for stabilizing the fish in the water, preventing pitching, and for steering the head up or down in straight swimming. The median dorsal and anal fins act in the same way as the keel of a boat, preventing rolling in the water, and the caudal (tail) fin is the principal means of propulsion and steering, used in the same way as a scull on a boat. Fins may be modified from this basic arrangement in various ways. In a few species the paired fins are more fleshy and can be used for 'crawling' on the bottom. The pectoral fins of the flying fish *(Exocoetoidei)* are greatly enlarged into wings enabling the

The brain is extremely small, and is connected, via the spinal cord, by ten pairs of nerves to the organs. Although this is extremely simple compared with higher vertebrates, the nervous system of the fish represents a considerable advance on the nervous organization of creatures immediately beneath it in the evolutionary sequence.

Respiration is generally by means of gills, which are situated behind the head underneath the opercula. Water is usually taken in through the mouth and passes over the gills before being expelled backwards from underneath the operculum, but this process may be reversed in fishes that habitually lie on the bottom, or the position of the gills may be shifted dorsally. Some groups of fishes have developed real lungs, particularly species which live in warm muddy water where oxygen is in short supply. In the catfish *Saccobranchus*, and *Clarias* there is a muscular air sac which extends along the body, and in *Amia* and *Lepisosteus* a honeycombed structure where exchange of gases also takes place. In *Misgurnis fossilis* it is the intestine which is modified to provide a lung.

The blood system consists of a small two-chambered heart, from which blood passes into the gill arches to be oxygenated and thence around the simple circulatory system and back to the heart. The main branches of blood vessels serve the regular locomotive muscle of the back and tail, and the gut, gonads and kidneys.

The digestive system is short, compared with higher vertebrates. It consists of mouth, pharynx, stomach, and intestine passing directly to the anus. The branchial arches are more or less involved in feeding, since in plankton-feeders they often have filtering combs on the inner side which help to strain out plankton from the water passing over the gills. The stomach is divided into two halves; in the first, sac-like part, whole food may often be found since fishes usually bolt their food in one piece. The second part may have more or fewer diverticula emptying into it, which are thought to aid digestion.

The kidneys and gonads share common ducts. A wide range of sexual forms are found among fishes, from hermaphrodite (having both male and female organs in the same individual) to separate sexes. There may be marked sexual dimorphism in some species, especially in the breeding season. Eggs and sperm are usually discharged directly into the water, but in some cases internal fertilization is the rule, and rarely the eggs are retained within the body of the female until they are ready to hatch or even after hatching. The care bestowed on the eggs also varies from casual abandonment of thousands of eggs to vigilant care of eggs deposited in a specially constructed nest.

The development and shape of the fish body is influenced, above all, by its environment. The general limitations and influence of moving, breathing and feeding in a watery medium have led to the common features shown by nearly all fishes: their streamlined shape, functional gills, scaly skin and methods of swimming. A consideration of environment must also take into account factors such as temperature, gas content and chemical composition of the water, as well as nature of the bottom and of the shore and additional influences in the form of other mammals and plants.

There are four main environment groups of fishes: those living exclusively in salt water; the ones living exclusively in fresh water; species spending part of their lives in salt and part in fresh water; and finally the group which is tolerant of both fresh and salt water and is frequently found in brackish water.

Marine fishes may be free-swimming (pelagic), or living on the sea bed (benthic). Benthic fishes may live either in deep water or shallow coastal waters. Freshwater species can be divided into river (rheophilous) types and still water (limnophilous) ones. There are also pelagic and benthic freshwater species. Of the fishes which spend part of their lives in fresh and part in salt water, there are the anadromous ones, such as the salmon and sea trout, which develop in fresh water and spend their adult, feeding, life in the sea, returning to freshwater to breed. The opposite pattern is found in, for example, the eel, which breeds in the sea and reaches maturity in freshwater; the eel is therefore said to be catadromous. Brackish-water species include the carp, roach and pike.

Let us first deal with running water as an environment. The whole of a river or stream does not contain the same collection of species along its whole course as might appear to be the case at first sight. Each part differs from the others in speed of flow, nature of the bed, and available cover, and can be divided into various sections, or zones. A watercourse generally includes, in order from its source, the spring, mountain brook, brook or river below the mountains, lowland river, and estuary or delta. In every main section the temperature, oxygen content, gradient, fauna and current will be different. The spring rarely contains much in the way of fishes, sometimes supporting bullheads or the odd trout. The mountain stream may contain minnows, stone loach, trout, and sometimes chubb. Most of these are found below the mountain, however, along with grayling, barbel, bleak, gudgeon, vimba, näsling and huchen. The lowland river reaches contain the richest fauna, including a number of cyprinids such as carp, bream, roach and bleak, as well as pike, catfish, pike-perch, and others. In the estuaries, where the water gradually changes from fresh to salt, there are all the species which are more or less tolerant of brackish water, including herring, sturgeon, sole and other flatfishes.

Water temperature has a great deal of influence on the speed of body processes, from general activity to rate of maturing. Different species vary widely in their tolerance of changing temperature, and tropical fishes tend on the whole to be less resistant to extreme fluctuations than fishes in more temperate waters. On the other hand, fishes seem to be better able to cope with colder water than warmer water. Most European species cannot tolerate a temperature higher than 37°C (98.6°F), having an optimum temperature of about 15—25°C (60—77°F). Special cases do occur, such as *Cyprinodon macularius* which lives in hot springs and can tolerate a temperature over 42°C (108°F), and, at the other extreme, *Dallia pectoralis*, which freezes for months at a time in the water in which it lives without any ill-effects. Seasonal fluctuations in temperature occur regularly within the optimum range, and the effect of these is usually to increase the torpidity of the fishes with lowering of temperature, when they feed less and may even hibernate. An exception to this rule is found in the burbot, which reaches a peak of activity and feeding with the advent of winter. Spawning in the burbot takes place between December and March, in the coldest months, and when, in summer, the water temperature rises above 25°C (77°F) the fish falls into a state of lethargy, a sort of aestivation.

The breeding habits of fishes are extremely varied. As a rule, the number of eggs laid increases with decreasing parental care; cod and herring are very prolific — one female may lay more than 28 million eggs — which they deposit in the open water and then ignore; salmon and trout — laying about 15,000 eggs — deposit their spawn in scooped-out holes in gravel or loose sand and then cover it over; bullheads — laying only a few hundred eggs — stick them to the underside of stones and guard them. The bitterling takes great trouble with its eggs. The female has a long ovipositor with which she is able to inject her eggs into the mantle cavity of freshwater mussels; she lays only 5—10 eggs. Eggs may be deposited on stones, plants, sand and gravel, in shells of molluscs, left to develop floating in swiftly-flowing water, or scattered indiscriminately.

Apart from long-term adaptations, fishes show a great deal of adaptability in their coloration. Some species are very brightly coloured, at least appearing to be so out of the water though in their natural habitat they may be difficult to distinguish. Not only does the colouring blend with the normal habitat, but it may also be possible for the fish to change colour as it moves from one place to another. It would be hard to find two individual trout of exactly the same colour; they range from light, silvery specimens in mountain streams to dark bluish-purple or black specimens in dark forest streams and pools. Dark trout placed experimentally in a light coloured vessel 'bleach' quite quickly, showing that they are reacting directly to the colour of their surroundings. Perch and roach respond similarly, although they are not apparently, in a wild state, very varied.

Direct reactions to other environmental conditions are not so rapid as colour-changes. For example, from experiments on trout it has been shown that young fish raised at lower temperatures tend to increase the number of vertebrae, fin rays and scales, which is apparently a direct effect of temperature on the developing embryo. The trout is known in three forms; sea trout, brook trout and lake trout. These forms have different modes of life and appearances that were once considered enough to separate them into species, but experiments on transferring them into different environments have shown that the differences between the three forms are due to acclimatization to their different habitats.

Fish and Man

Fish have always formed an important part of man's diet. Fishbones have been found in association with the remains of prehistoric man, and he seems to have learned very quickly to make fishhooks as soon as material was available for this purpose. Testimony is also found in the sculptures of ancient Egypt and Assyria, in the ancient history of China, and in the oldest written records of many continents and civilizations. The Greeks and Romans were passionate anglers.

Although the people of ancient times in some places lived almost entirely on fish, they must have been mystified by such questions as where the shoals go to spawn, what makes them move around from one fishing ground to another, or even apparently disappear for some part of the year. Fishing was not a mechanical art, but depended on knowing where the fish were, and so man learned about their habits, spawning, shelters and stations, their travels upstream and downstream.

Progress in fishing methods began with the construction of dams and simple obstacles, primitive bownets and fishpots. The net represented a big step forward, since it enabled a man to catch more fish than he needed for his own use so that he could exchange them for other articles. Population growth and social and cultural development have brought, together with the increased demand, improvements in fishing technique, transport and storage. Coastal communities have ranged farther afield in search of fishing grounds, but in continental countries, particularly those with little or no coastline, it has been necessary to develop fish culture, stocking artificial reservoirs with edible fish. In Europe alone this industry is 800 years old, and it is well known that the ancient Chinese were successful fish breeders. In the works of Varro, a Roman writer, there are references to artificial reservoirs built by rich Roman patricians for keeping fish, and Columella recorded that the Romans not only kept fish but also bred them.

It is certain that the demand for fish breeding, keeping and catching will continue to develop. Even though in recent years the world yield has increased considerably, it is not sufficient to cover the world requirements. The economic importance of fish is equivalent to the annual production of beef.

Not only do fish provide a source of relatively cheap food, but fish flesh is nutritiously valuable, particularly digestible with its albumin content and having a mineral content in some ways superior to red meat. All fishes contain a high level of phosphorus, and all marine fishes have a great deal of iodine. The pike and salmonid fishes are rich in calcium and vitamins A and D.

Nearly every part of a fish can be used for something. Apart from delicacies such as caviare of fish roe, vitamin-rich oil from the liver of some fishes, the bones can be used for fertilizers or glue. In Japan even the intestines are used in making string, and guanine can be extracted from the scales of cyprinids for use in artificial pearl manufacturing.

Although we remove an enormous quantity of fish from the oceans of the world, the resources have not been exhausted and, if properly used, the sea can provide food in quantities far beyond the amount we are able to grow on the surface of the land.

No discussion of fishes would be complete without some mention of the pursuit of angling. To find the origins of this sport one would have to go back to times before written records. It is possible that prehistoric man, with his primitive fishhooks, may have known the same thrill of feeling a 'bite' as modern anglers using sophisticated equipment. Nowadays, angling is highly organized, hedged about with close seasons and codes of conduct which make it a relaxing and stimulating leisure-time occupation for thousands of members of angling clubs. Practically every piece of running and still water in the British Isles belongs to someone or somebody that has the fishing rights. The great exception to this rule is the River Thames below the Town Stone at Staines which was presented to the citizens of London for all time by Richard II.

PLATES

The Sterlet

Acipenser ruthenus LINNAEUS, 1758

The Sturgeons are a very ancient and, when compared with other fishes, also a very primitive family, whose origin can be traced back to the Palaeozoic and Mesozoic, i.e. some 500 million years back.

They have an elongated, spindle-shaped body terminating in an asymmetrical caudal fin, and the head protrudes into a very long snout (rostrum) with a ventral mouth.

The characteristic Sturgeon body is covered with bony scutes arranged in five rows. The dorsal row numbers 10—17 scutes, the lateral rows 52—71, the abdominal 10—19. The dorsal fin has 37—54 rays, the anal fin 19—31 rays. The snout is of varying length. In front of the protrusible mouth there are four fringed barbels, the lower jaw is cleft. The coloration of the Sterlet varies from greenish hues through brown to bright pink.

The Sterlet is the only European member of the Sturgeon family living in fresh water all the year round. It spawns in rivers with clean, stony bottom, the spawning season extending from the middle of April to the middle of June. In the spawning season the Sterlet has a characteristic whitish cover on the head. It lays between 4 and 140 thousand eggs. The Sterlet may live to an age of 22 or more years, attaining a length of $2\frac{1}{2}$ feet and a weight of 5 lbs at the age of 15 years. Its maximum length is about 4 ft and the maximum weight 35 lbs.

The Sterlet lives in the rivers emptying into the Black, Caspian, White and Kara Seas. Experiments have been made with its acclimatization in fish ponds, where the Sterlet grows exceedingly well, but never reproduces.

In some rivers, such as the Volga, the Don and the Dnieper the Sterlet is abundant, some 500 tons being caught every year. It has very tasty flesh which can be eaten fresh, frozen or smoked.

(H.)

Mr Holčík's texts are marked (H.)

Mr Mihálik's texts are marked (M.)

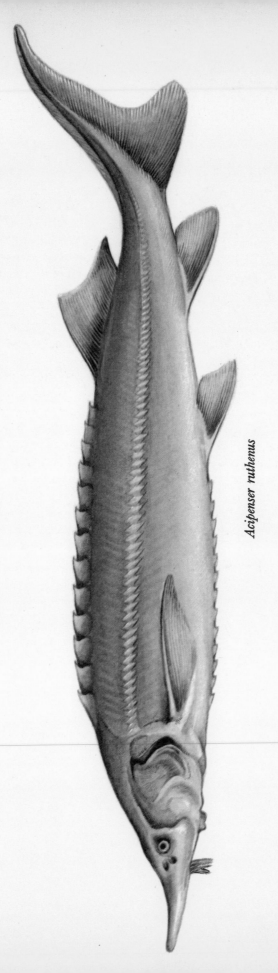

Acipenser ruthenus

The Common Sturgeon

Acipenser sturio LINNAEUS, 1758

The Common Sturgeon is the only sturgeon living in Western Europe. In the past it was very numerous, but now, however, it is very quickly disappearing despite its being protected all the year round.

Its elongate spindle-shaped body is covered with large bony scutes arranged in five rows. The dorsal row numbers 9—13 scutes, the lateral ones 24—35 each. The dorsal and anal fins are set far back, the former containing 31—43 rays, the latter 22—26 rays. The characteristic head projects into a rostrum with four preoral barbels and a large remarkably protrusible mouth.

As with the majority of sturgeons, the Common Sturgeon is a migratory fish. It lives in the sea when mature, entering fresh water only in the spawning season, i.e. in Spring and Summer. It spawns in large rivers depositing its eggs straight into the water where they sink to the gravelly bottom. The number of eggs laid by one female Sturgeon is considerable — the ovaries of an adult female contain 1—6 millions. After hatching, the young Sturgeons slowly float down to the sea. The Sturgeon feeds mostly on small invertebrate animals and smaller fishes, attaining a length of up to 10 ft and a weight of 650 lbs.

The Common Sturgeon is the only representative of the Sturgeon family *(Acipenseridae)* in Western Europe, in the North from North Cape as far as the Baltic Sea, the Mediterranean and the Black Seas. It is also found along the Atlantic coast of North America from Hudson Bay to South Carolina, and occurs rarely in Iceland. Its present economic importance is almost nil, as it is caught only rarely. In 1930—1939 the world annual yield was about 130 tons at the most.

(H.)

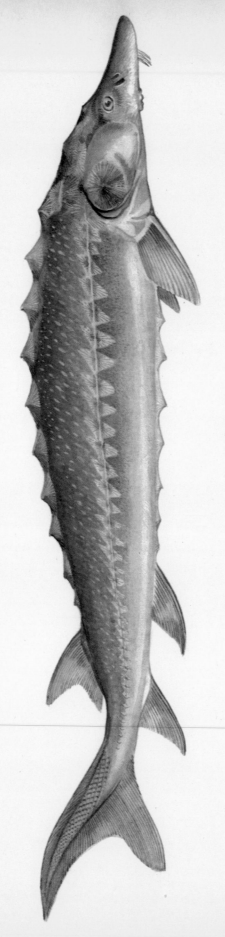

Acipenser sturio

The Salmon

Salmo salar LINNAEUS, 1758

There is no fish more beautiful and more interesting than the salmon which has always been and still remains the dream of every angler. Its strong, torpedo-shaped body, its mysterious life now in the sea, now in the fresh water of rivers or streams, its almost inexhaustible energy in overcoming obstacles during its ascent upstream, its gameness when caught on the hook and, last but not least, the extraordinary quality and taste of its flesh — all these factors result in its common reputation — the royal fish.

In appearance the Salmon resembles its near relative, the Sea Trout, for which it is often mistaken. Its dorsal fin has 3—5 hard and 9—12 soft rays, the anal fin containing 3—4 hard and 7—10 soft rays. The lateral line comprises some 114—130 small scales, the first branchial arch bears 17—24 gill rakers. The caudal fin is always more or less forked. The flanks below the lateral line either have a very small number of black spots or none at all. The spots, if present, are cruciform and occur only on the anterior half of the body as far as the end of the base of the dorsal fin. Adult Salmon living in the sea are silvery steel-blue. During their ascent for spawning the colour, particularly of the male specimens, becomes darker. At that time the male is bronze to reddish brown, with red spots appearing among the usual black ones. Apart from that the lower jaw of the male elongates and bends upwards in a hook-like fashion while no such change occurs in the female. The colour of the young in the "parr" phase, before they leave their hatching place for the sea, is similar to that of the Trout or the Sea Trout, the body showing 8—13 transverse dark spots. In the "smolt" phase, i.e. during its descent downstream into the sea, the Salmon is silvery.

The mature Salmon lives in the sea. It is hatched, however, in fresh water and stays in the river for some time afterwards, returning there again for spawning. The ascent of the Salmon to their spawning grounds usually occurs in two waves. The first, usually consisting of smaller specimens, starts upstream at the end of Spring and in Summer; the other larger fishes appear in the spawning places at the end of the Summer and in the Autumn. The fishes of the first wave spawn in the Autumn of the year of their arrival, while the second group, including mostly females, spends the winter in the river to spawn next Spring. During its ascent of the rivers to the spawning places the Salmon usually does not take any food, it is capable of overcoming obstacles of the most varied kind, such as waterfalls, weirs, etc., as much as 10 ft high or even higher. The adult female lays 4—27 thousand eggs

Salmo salar — male

The Salmon - *continued*

about half of which remain unfertilized. Spawning takes place on gravelly and stony riverbeds, in which the female makes a nest by vigorously jerking her powerful tail. In this nest she deposits the eggs and when they have been fertilized by the male she covers them with sand. Most Salmon spawn only once or twice in their lives. Many of them, particularly the males, die immediately after spawning, the remaining ones dying of exhaustion or disease on their return to the sea. There is only one case known of a female which spawned five times during the eight years of her life. The young hatch in the Spring, in May, continuing to live in the same stream or the river for one to five years (the "parr" phase of their development).

After this period they become silvery and drift down to the sea (the "smolt" phase). Thanks to abundant food consisting mostly of herrings, fishes of the genus of *Ammodytes*, molluscs, etc., and their extraordinary voracity they grow very quickly in the sea, the annual weight increase amounting to as much as 11 lbs. When hunting for food they undertake long journeys, often travelling as far as 150 miles in 16 days.

The length of their stay in the sea varies. Some of them, particularly the males, return to the rivers after one year in the sea; the majority of them, however, return after two years. Their growth in the sea is very rapid; within three months they can attain a length of 3 ft. Some of the fishes, mostly males, remain in the river all their lives, and having matured they spawn together with the other Salmon from the sea. The growth of these specimens is slower, up to a length of 1 ft at the most. The usual maximum length of a Salmon is 4—5 ft or more, and it may weigh some 85 lbs. The heaviest salmon ever caught (England, 1902) weighed 103 lbs.

The Salmon is found on both sides of the Atlantic. In Europe its range extends from the West Coast of Portugal, the Bay of Biscay, to the North and Baltic Sea, the Scandinavian coast as far as the Arctic Ocean and the White Sea; in America it covers the whole Atlantic coast as far south as the Hudson River, Greenland, and Iceland. In large lakes, and sometimes in rivers, there is a non-migratory variety — *Salmo salar* m. *sebago*.

The Salmon affords anglers unforgettable memories; it is caught most frequently near estuaries during its ascent for spawning. The quality of its flesh is exquisite (apart from the "kelt", i.e. those returning to the sea after spawning). It is by right, therefore, that the salmon is considered to be one of our most valuable fishes.

(H.)

Salmo salar — female

The Sea Trout

Salmo trutta LINNAEUS, 1758

The Sea Trout differs from the Salmon in its more sturdy body. The caudal peduncle is stronger than that of the Salmon, and the caudal fin is truncated or only slightly forked. The number of scales between the lateral line and the adipose fin is smaller than in the Salmon, and the arrangement of the gills is different, the number of gill rakers on the first branchial arch being lower (13—18) than in the Salmon (17—24). The number of hard rays in the dorsal fin is the same as in the Salmon (three), the number of soft rays varying between 8 and 11; the anal fin has 2 or 3 hard and 8 or 9 soft rays. The lateral line includes 118—120 small scales. In general the Sea Trout is characterized by its silvery colour when in the sea and a richer, darker hue in the spawning season and during its stay in the rivers. The sides of the body below and above the lateral line are covered with black, often cruciform spots. In mature males numerous pink or red spots appear in the spawning season. The colouring of the young is identical to that of young Brown Trout: on the flanks there are distinct transverse stripes mostly bluish in colour.

The males differ from the females in the distinctly hooked lower maxillary bone. The hook is not, however, as pronounced as in the Salmon.

The Sea Trout is a migratory (anadromous) species. When mature it lives in the sea, and during the spawning season it ascends the rivers. Its migration has a mass, seasonal character. As in the Salmon, there are two varieties, the spring one and the autumn one. In Scotland most of the Sea Trout belong to the spring variety, coming to the spawning places in spring or summer and spawning in the autumn of the same year. The rest belong to the autumn variety, arriving at the spawning places at the end of the summer or in the autumn and spawning the next year. The main spawning season covers October and November. With vigorous strokes of its tail the female makes a "nest" in the gravelly river bottom with a length of several feet and depth up to 3 feet, into which she deposits her eggs, covering them with sand, gravel and stones after fertilization. The hatched young

Salmo trutta — male

The Sea Trout - *continued*

do not leave the river immediately, but develop in fresh water near where they hatched for a shorter or longer period (the "parr" phase). Sea Trout of English and Scottish rivers normally leave fresh water after two or three years, the Norwegian after 3 years, the Swedish after 3 or 4 years, the White Sea after 4 years, and some of them e.g. those living in the rivers of North Sweden, do not leave fresh water for 5—7 years. Not all fishes however, descend the rivers to the sea. A very small number (1 or 2%) remain in fresh water permanently and mature there. These specimens, mostly males, are almost identical with the Brown Trout with which they usually interbreed. The descent to the sea (the "smolt") usually begins in the spring, in April or May, when the fishes are 4—8 ins long. In the sea the Sea Trout does not range as far as the Salmon, usually keeping near the coast and estuaries. Its growth in the sea proceeds much more slowly than that of the Salmon. In the fourth year the Sea Trout attains a length of 20—30 ins. Its diet in the sea consists of herrings, sprats and molluscs.

The length of its stay in the sea varies. Often it returns to the rivers in the Autumn of the year it left them (whitling), particularly the males. Most frequently, however, it returns to fresh water after two years in the sea, and this period may be even longer (up to five years). The Sea Trout lays some 5—9 thousand eggs. It is generally smaller than the Salmon, with a length of 1 or 2 ft and weighing 2—10 lbs. The heaviest specimen so far caught by fair angling in the British Isles (Scotland, 1866) weighed $39\frac{1}{2}$ lbs.

The Sea Trout occurs in the same localities as the Salmon, i.e. along the sea coast of Europe from the river Duero in Spain to the White Sea in the North of the USSR, and in the Baltic Sea.

The Sea Trout is a valued angling and industrial fish, its very tasty, fat flesh being highly appreciated.

(H.)

Salmo trutta — female

The Brown Trout (or the Brook Trout)

Salmo trutta m. *fario* LINNAEUS, 1758

The Brown Trout, this inhabitant of cold mountain streams with a high oxygen content, is second perhaps in popularity only to the Carp, its great variability of coloration making it the most exotic of the European freshwater fishes.

Its strong, cylindrical, yet slender body betrays the fact that it is a good swimmer. Its coloration is so varied that even in the same water it is impossible to find two similar specimens. Its general colour is brown with green or blue hues, but rich mauve to almost black specimens are not infrequent. Its back and flanks are covered with black and red spots, mostly with pale blue, orange or yellowish rims. Its strong fins are usually darker, sometimes, however, paler. The dorsal fin has 3—5 hard and 9—11 soft rays, the anal fin 2—4 hard and 7—9 soft rays. The lateral line contains 115—132 small scales firmly embedded in the skin. The caudal fin is large, only slightly forked, in older specimens truncated or even rounded. The male differs from the female in having a more deeply cleft mouth and a hooked lower maxillary bone. However, this mouth shape is far less pronounced in the Brown Trout than in the Salmon and the Sea Trout.

The Brown Trout is a relative of the Sea Trout. It has already lost its migratory instinct, however, and remains in rivers and streams all its life without undertaking any long journeys. In the past this fact was the subject of long disputes which were finally resolved by a very simple experiment: the Sea Trout was bred in ponds or other fresh waters from which it could not escape, where it was seen to mature after a certain time, and to spawn and yield the young. These were perfectly capable of living, but had partly lost their migratory instinct, which disappeared entirely in the following generations. On the other hand, the common Brown Trout, bred in estuaries or actually in the sea, changes into the Sea Trout after some time, showing a strong migratory instinct. It is known, for example, that Brown Trout introduced and acclimatized in the short rivers of New Zealand, often found their way into the sea and changed into the migratory Sea Trout shortly afterwards. That the Brown Trout is nothing but a fresh water form of the Sea Trout is also borne out by the fact that in places with no Sea Trout, there are not, and have never been any Brown Trout.

The Brown Trout is a typical cold water fish inhabiting mostly mountain rivers and brooks, but often living in lowland rivers and brooks provided they have a clean, gravelly

Salmo trutta — m. fario male

The Brown Trout (or the Brook Trout) - *continued*

bottom, clean and not very warm water and a high level of dissolved oxygen. It occurs also in ponds, lakes and reservoirs, particularly if the flow of water through them is sufficient. In mountain waters it often ascends to considerable altitudes, as high as 8300 ft above sea level.

In these rivers and streams, with abundant cold, oxygen saturated water, but with very little food, the Brown Trout is often the only inhabitant. The breeding behaviour of the Brown Trout is similar to that of its relatives, the Salmon and the Sea Trout. It spawns at the end of Autumn or early Winter, most frequently in October to December, in mountain brooks with clean, unsoiled sand or gravel. In the spawning season the Brown Trout ascends a little way from lower to higher places or tributaries, often overcoming obstacles in the manner characteristic of the family. As with the Salmon and the Sea Trout in the spawning season, the female hides the fertilized eggs at the bottom of the stream, covering them with sand, thus protecting them from damage or enemies. One female lays about 200—1500 eggs (about 500—1000 eggs being 1 lb of its weight). The orange coloured eggs are relatively large. The young hatch after about 20 days at 1—2°C, higher water temperatures naturally speeding the hatching period. After hatching, the embryo is just under an inch long. At first it hides among the stones, but after it has consumed its yolk-sac, which does not last more than 20 days, it must begin to lead an independent life. It feeds on microscopic animals suspended in water or stuck to the stones, beginning with small prey and, as it grows, feeding on larger creatures. The food of adult Brown Trout consists mostly of the benthos, i.e. animals living at the bottom of watercourses, including insect larvae, crustaceans of the *Gammarus* genus, small molluscs, insects trapped in the water, fish eggs (often their own), small fishes, tadpoles and even frogs. Large specimens even catch and devour small mammals (shrews, field mice, etc.). The type and quantity of food, as well as the environment in which the fish lives, influence its rate of growth and final size. Thus Trout living in high mountain brooks with little food rarely attain angling length, usually being only 6—8 ins long. In normal conditions the Brown Trout attains a length of about 3 ins in its first year, 4—7 ins in the second, 6—8 ins in the third, and 7—9 ins in the fourth year, when it weighs 5—7 ozs. In very good conditions the growth of the

Salmo trutta m. *fario* — female and young

The Brown Trout (or the Brook Trout) - *continued*

Brown Trout is fairly rapid as it weighs 1 lb in about two or three years. Very useful information on the biology and the growth potential of the Trout has been acquired through experimental breeding in a reservoir. The fishes put into the reservoir remained in still water and adjusted themselves to the conditions, ascending the tributaries only for spawning. The spawning season over, the fishes returned to the reservoir. With the large number of small fishes in the reservoir the Trout grew very quickly. In the first year they attained a length of 4 ins and a weight of $\frac{1}{2}$ oz, in the second year 7 ins and 3 oz, in the third $12\frac{1}{2}$ ins and $1\frac{1}{4}$ lbs, in the fourth 16 ins, and $2\frac{1}{2}$ lbs, in the fifth 20 ins and 5 lbs, in in the sixth 2 ft and 10 lbs, and in the seventh $2\frac{1}{2}$ ft and 15 lbs. They lost their original "brook" coloration, becoming silvery or slightly speckled. The original coloration returned only during the spawning season. One of these fishes is represented on Fig. 9 showing a Trout from the Klíčava Reservoir (14 ins, $1\frac{3}{4}$ lbs). This male was captured twice; once in September, 1964, when it had uniform silvery colouring with a small number of black spots and no red ones; it was caught for the second time exactly one month later. At that time it was ready for spawning, the colouring having changed to that shown in our illustration.

As a rule the Brown Trout lives for about 12 years. However, a case is known of a Trout which lived in a well for exactly 49 years, although — due to shortage of food — it was only $1\frac{1}{2}$ feet long. The usual average weight of Trout is about 1 lb, specimens of 2—10 lbs being caught only rarely. In exceptional cases, however, a Trout may weigh 25—40 lbs.

The Brown Trout lives in Western Europe, its habitat extending from the Murmansk coast and Iceland to the Mediterranean, the Balkans, Asia Minor, North Africa (Morocco, Algeria) and Iran. From Europe it has been introduced into America, New Zealand, Japan and elsewhere.

It is appreciated, above all, for its gameness, trout fishing being highly valued as a sport affording real pleasure to anglers. It has also considerable economic importance as it can be kept in fish ponds, either specially reserved for trout keeping, in which case it must be fed, or combined carp and trout ponds, particularly at higher altitudes where the keeping of carp alone would be unprofitable.

(H.)

Salmo trutta m. fario — Brook Trout changing into Lake Trout

The Lake Trout

Salmo trutta m. *lacustris* LINNAEUS, 1758

In the still fresh water of lakes, Sea Trout as well as Brown (Brook) Trout easily adjust themselves to their new living conditions and form a non-migratory variety known as the Lake Trout; this is not a separate species, however, as many anglers believe.

The Lake Trout is almost identical with the Sea Trout and the Brown Trout. It differs from the two latter forms only in its sturdier body and its coloration. Its basic colour is silvery, silver grey or bluish. Its back is more intensely coloured than its flanks, being often of a bluish or greenish hue. The flanks and particularly the back are covered with large black spots, orange or pink spots appearing only infrequently. Paler specimens are usually small immature fish living in the upper layers of water, the darker speckled specimens being mature individuals living in deep water.

The Lake Trout lives in the cold, deep waters of Alpine, Scandinavian, and Scottish lakes. Its spawning is similar to that of the Sea Trout or Brown Trout, taking place in the Autumn and at the beginning of Winter, mostly in the tributaries of the lakes, exceptionally directly under the clean, gravelly lake banks at a depth of 13—16 ft. After hatching, the young live in the brooks where they were born for 2 or 3 years, afterwards floating down to the lake. The fish grow more in the lakes than in the brooks. Although during the three years of its life in the brook the young Lake Trout attains a length of 7—10 ins, in the course of a single year in the lake it can grow to a length of over 20 ins. The young feed mostly on invertebrates, adult trout being predatory on roach, char, white-fish, frequently even minnows. The female grows more quickly than the male, maturing in the 4th—6th year, the male usually maturing one year earlier. In good feeding conditions the Lake Trout may even attain a weight of 40—50 lbs, normally reaching a length of 3 ft and a weight of 20 lbs, generally at an age of ten years.

The Lake Trout occurs chiefly in lakes which are or were at some time connected with the basins inhabited by the Sea Trout or the Brown Trout, including the lakes of Switzerland, Austria, Scandinavia, England and Scotland, up to about 500 ft above sea level.

It is a fish of considerable economic importance, caught on the hook by anglers and in nets for industrial purposes.

(H.)

Salmo trutta m. lacustris — male

The Rainbow Trout

Salmo gairdneri irideus GIBBONS, 1855

The name "Rainbow Trout" includes not just one, but several species of North American trout characterized by black spots scattered all over the body and a red or purple band along the flanks. The original habitat of these species, which can be classified into several groups, is the Atlantic coast of North America from South Alaska to Mexico. The species includes migratory and non-migratory forms. The migratory forms live in the sea ascending the rivers only for spawning, and the non-migratory ones live in fresh water all their lives. The Americans distinguish three main groups of the Rainbow Trout, the Rainbow Trout, the Steelhead, and the Cut-Throat forms. From its original habitat the Rainbow Trout has spread to other regions of the USA. In 1882 it was introduced into Europe (Germany), in 1883-84 into New Zealand, Tasmania, and Australia, in 1889 to South Africa and in 1926 to Madagascar. In 1877 it was successfully acclimatized in Japan. All Rainbow Trout acclimatized in Europe and probably also elsewhere were produced by cross-breeding of migratory and non-migratory forms, most probably the *Salmo shasta* (non-migratory) and the *Salmo gairdneri* (migratory) species. This is borne out chiefly by the fact that the acclimatized Rainbow Trout very often disappears from fresh waters and appears on the sea coast. Such cases have frequently been observed in Europe, particularly in the coastal waters of Denmark and Germany. This is also the reason why attempts to introduce and acclimatize the Rainbow Trout have failed so often.

The mature Rainbow Trout is easily distinguished from the Brown Trout or the Char by its thick-set body almost covered with a large number of black spots extending as far as the dorsal and caudal fins. Its most marked characteristic, however, is the red or purple band running along its flanks in the middle of the body. The coloration of the males, particularly in the spawning season, is very vivid greyish-black with a rich mauve lustre. The females and all those living in stagnant water are paler. The dorsal fin contains 4 hard and 9 or 10 soft rays, the anal fin 3 hard and 10 or 11 soft rays. The lateral line comprises 120—150 small scales.

Salmo gairdneri irideus — male in the spawning season

The Rainbow Trout - *continued*

The immature Rainbow Trout is similar to the young of the Brown Trout, differing from the latter only in the higher density of its black spots and the absence of red spots. The males, apart from richer colouring, differ from the females in their more deeply cleft mouth and marked curvature of the lower maxillary bone. The body of fishes from still water is relatively shorter and higher than that of fishes living in rivers and streams.

The Rainbow Trout lives in both still and running water. It prefers cold water, but — contrary to the Brown Trout — endures relatively high temperatures so that it is often bred in ponds, usually together with Carp. As a rule, its spawning season begins with the departure of ice, in February and March in southerly regions and in May and June in northern regions, being at its height in March and April. A female lays 500 to 3000 eggs (about 800 to 1000 eggs being 1 lb of its weight) which she conceals, after their fertilization, in sand or gravel. The development of the eggs takes $1\frac{1}{2}$—2 months, according to the temperature of the water. In the first year the young Rainbow Trout grows to a length of 3—5 ins, in the second year 5—9 ins, and in the third 8—11 ins. A mature specimen measures 20—36 ins and weighs up to 12 lbs, the usual weight being 1—$2\frac{1}{2}$ lbs. The biggest Rainbow Trout ever caught (in the USA) weighed 35 lbs. In ponds, lakes and reservoirs, where it usually has more food than in rivers and brooks, it grows more quickly, attaining a weight of 4 lbs in its fourth year. It feeds on crustaceans, molluscs, larvae of aquatic insects, insects that have fallen into the water, and larger specimens also eat smaller fishes.

In 1882 the Rainbow Trout was brought from the USA to Europe and acclimatized, spreading gradually all over Europe. It is kept mostly in still water, particularly where its escape to the sea can be prevented.

The Rainbow Trout attracts anglers by its gameness, beautiful appearance and, last but not least, its exotic origin. It is caught on the fly or by trailing, the latter method being used chiefly in high season. It is often kept in ponds with carps, the combination enabling better use of the natural potential of the pond and higher yields.

(H.)

38

Salmo gairdneri irideus — female from a fish pond breed

The Char

Salvelinus alpinus (LINNAEUS, 1758)

The Char is a salmonid fish living in the seas and fresh waters of Europe, North America and North Asia. It differs from the genus *Salmo* in the dentition of its palatal bones. The only marine Char occurs along the European coast.

One of the characteristics of the Char is the large number of small scales in its lateral line which amounts to 130—140. Its dorsal fin has 3 or 4 hard and 8—11 soft rays, the anal fin 3 or 4 hard and 7 or 8 soft rays. The first branchial arch has 18—30 gill rakers. Another typical feature of the Char is its deeply cleft mouth, the upper maxillary bone extending past the vertical tangent to the hind part of the eye. The colouring of the Char is very rich, placing it among the most beautiful salmonids. In the spawning season the back is blue, the flanks greenish blue or green, covered with small circular red or orange spots, the belly bright red and bright yellow below the mouth. The front edge of the red pectoral fins, ventral fins and anal fin is milky white, the dorsal and caudal fins being of the same colour as the back. Out of the spawning season the colouring is paler and the belly silvery.

The Char is a typical cold water migratory fish characteristic of arctic regions. It lives in the sea when mature and breeds and spends the first years of its life in rivers, not ascending, however, as high as the Salmon or the Sea Trout. Biologically it is similar to the Salmon and the Sea Trout. The Char attains a length of up to $3\frac{1}{2}$ ft and a weight of up to 32 lbs. As a rule specimens are caught measuring some $1\frac{1}{2}$ ft long and weighing 2—3 lbs.

The Char is a circumpolar species living in the seas and the rivers of Greenland, Iceland, North Norway (above 65° North), Bear Island, Spitsbergen, Novaya Zemlya, the Siberian coast, arctic Canada and Hudson Bay. It does not occur in the Baltic Sea, but the lakes of Swedish Lapland are the habitat of a fresh water form not very different from the sea form.

As it is found in larger numbers only in the extreme North, the Char is exploited chiefly in these regions. It is a favourite with anglers, the quality of its flesh being similar to that of the Sea Trout.

(H.)

Salvelinus alpinus — male

The Alpine Char

Salvelinus salvelinus (LINNAEUS, 1758)

The various glacial lakes of the Alps, North Norway, Ireland, Scotland, Shetland and Orkney Islands and Iceland are the habitat of about 30 more species and forms of the Char. The systematic classification of these species, their relationships and particularly their differentiation are insufficiently understood. Almost every lake harbours a different form or variety, particularly in the lakes of Ireland, Scotland and England, where at least 15 species and varieties have so far been described. The best known among them is the Alpine Char which we include as the only representative of these freshwater Chars.

The Alpine Char has a trout-shaped, slender body with a forked caudal fin. Its dorsal fin has 3 hard and 12—15 soft rays, and the anal fin 3 hard and 11—13 soft rays. Its lateral line consists of 190—220 scales. The first branchial arch has at least 20 gill rakers. The back of the Alpine Char is greenish blue, its flanks pink, the belly yellow or pinkish. The back and the flanks are covered with yellowish spots of various sizes. The paired fins have a white front edge. The belly of the male is red.

The Alpine Char lives in cold, clean lakes up to 7000 ft above sea level. There are two forms, based on spawning season, one spawning in winter (November to January) laying its eggs on sand or gravel of lake banks, the other spawning in summer (July to August) depositing its eggs some 65 to 250 ft deep in the water. Other forms can be distinguished on the basis of differences in size, kind of food, etc., such as (1) the normal medium-sized form feeding on plankton and benthos, (2) the predatory form ("Wildfangsaibling") feeding on fish and attaining a weight of 8—10 lbs, (3) the "Schwarzreuter" form characteristic of the Alpine lakes with very little food to be found, a pygmy form attaining hardly a length of 4—6 ins and a weight of 3 ozs, feeding on plankton, (4) the deep water form ("Tiefseesaibling") living at a depth of 100—350 ft feeding on plankton and organisms found at the bottom of the lakes, growing to a length of only 4—8 ins.

The Alpine Char is, above all, valued by anglers, sometimes being also caught in nets. Its flesh is considered a delicacy. It is caught by fly-fishing, spinning or live baiting.

(H.)

Salvelinus salvelinus — male

The American Brook Trout

Salvelinus fontinalis MITCHILL, 1815

Apart from the Rainbow Trout Europe harbours another type of American salmonid, the American Brook Trout. It was imported to Europe for the first time in 1884, and then spread from Germany to other European countries. The American Brook Trout is one of the most beautiful fishes of the country of its origin.

The American Brook Trout differs from the Brown Trout in its more flattened body and its large, elongated head provided with a deeply cleft mouth reaching far beyond the vertical tangent of the eye and well stocked with teeth. The eyes are large and set above the centre line of the body. The dorsal fin contains 3—5 hard and 8—10 soft rays, the anal fin 3—5 hard and 7—9 soft rays. The lateral line numbers 109—130 scales, the first branchial arch incorporates 11—22 gill rakers. The colour range of the American Brook Trout is very wide and extraordinarily variable. The basic colour is olive green, marbled on the back, with the marbled pattern breaking up into irregular yellow, orange or red spots lower down the flanks. The belly is silvery, mauvish, but sometimes grey or orange, in mature males orange-red. The anal, ventral, and pectoral fins are red or orange, with a characteristic black and white margin on the front edge. The males differ from the females in their more vivid colouring and the hook-shaped curvature of their lower maxillary bone.

The American Brook Trout is a non-migratory fish living in cool, clean brooks and mountain streams with a high oxygen content. In America, however, a migratory form occurs, living in fresh water for 3 or 4 years after hatching, and then leaving for the sea. Lack of success in acclimatizing the American Brook Trout in many places (including England) can be explained by the fact that the migratory form has been chosen for this purpose. The breeding and other habits of the American Brook Trout are similar to those of the Brown Trout. Where the American Brook Trout and the European Brown Trout live together, they interbreed easily. The growth of the American Brook Trout is more rapid than that of the Brown Trout; it normally measures 12—16 ins and weighs 1 to 2 lbs. The heaviest specimen so far caught came from the river Nipigon in Canada (tributary of Lake Superior). It was 3 ft long and weighed $14\frac{1}{2}$ lbs.

The American Brook Trout is very popular with anglers; it is caught mostly on artificial fly. Sometimes it is kept in ponds.

(H.)

Salvelinus fontinalis — male

The Huchen

Hucho hucho (LINNAEUS, 1758)

The cold and swift streams and rivers below the mountains of Central and Eastern Europe are the habitat of a sturdy and strong salmonid fish which is famous for its strength and beauty — the Huchen. It is related to trout of the genus *Salvelinus*, but exceeds them in size, as it may weigh as much as 1000 lbs.

The Huchen is characterized, above all, by its slender, torpedo-shaped body. It has a large head, deeply cleft mouth well stocked with teeth, and typically large eyes. The dorsal fin has 3 or 4 hard and 9 or 10 soft rays, the anal fin 4 or 5 hard and 7—9 soft rays. The lateral line incorporates 180—200 scales; the number of gill rakers is only 10 or 11. The basic colour is brown to reddish brown with a greenish hue, changing into bright copper red on the flanks. The belly is bright yellow or grey. The young lack the brown colour, being silvery with transverse dark stripes.

The Huchen, living in the Danube basin, is a non-migratory fish, its characteristic habitat being the rivers below the mountains where it lives with Grayling, Barbel and Näsling. It lives in both deeper backwaters and pools and swift streams, where, however, it must have suitable shelter. It spawns in the spring, most frequently in April and May. Mature specimens weigh 3 lbs at 5—6 years. In the spawning season the Huchen travels high up the rivers in which it lives and enters even small brooks. The manner of spawning is similar to that of other salmonids. The food of adult Huchen consists mostly of large fish. The growth of the Huchen is very rapid: in its fifth year it can measure between 22 and 24 inches. Even in relatively small bodies of water it attains a weight of 20—40 lbs. The biggest fish ever caught came from the Danube and weighed 114½ lbs. In still water it grows and matures quickly, spawning, however, only in tributaries.

The Huchen is a characteristic inhabitant of the Danube river basin, being found also in the river Prut in Eastern Europe. It occurs most frequently in Czechoslovakia, Poland, and Rumania. From Czechoslovakia it is exported abroad, to North Africa (Morocco, Algeria) and other countries.

The Huchen is a very valuable salmonid fish popular with exacting anglers. It is caught by live baiting or trolling.

(H.)

46

Hucho hucho — male

The White-Fish

Coregonus albula LINNAEUS, 1758

The genus *Coregonus* includes a number of salmonid species of the Northern hemisphere. Their most important characteristic is relatively large scales, the lateral line numbering 111 scales at the most. Their jaws have no teeth or only very small filament teeth. The first branchial arch is provided with long gill rakers. From the large number of species living in Europe we will mention only a few of the more important, including the White-Fish.

At first sight it resembles our herring, only the presence of the adipose fin betraying its relationship with the salmonids. The dorsal fin has 3—5 hard rays and 8—10 soft rays, the anal fin 3 or 4 hard and 10—13 soft rays. The lateral line incorporates 70—91 scales, the gills have 36—52 gill rakers. The lower jaw is considerably longer than the upper jaw and turned upwards. The back is green or greenish blue, the flanks silvery, the dorsal, caudal and the adipose fins are greyish, and the remaining fins are colourless.

The White-Fish is a characteristic inhabitant of the so-called oligotrophic lakes (with little food to be found in them) with clear, pure, cold water and a coarse sandy or gravelly bottom. It is very sensitive to oxygen concentration, often changing its habitat in accordance with the saturation of water with oxygen. White-Fish congregate in large shoals living in summer mostly in the deeper open waters of the lakes. Towards autumn they rise and come to the shore. The spawning season is in the autumn, most frequently during October and November. The spawning places are usually at a depth of some 10 to 65 ft, in some Swedish lakes even 200—350 ft below the water level. The growth depends on the quantity of plankton which forms its staple food, and the density of its population. In the third year the White-Fish attains a length of 4—9 ins. The biggest White-Fish caught came from Poland. It was 12 years old, 15 ins long, and weighed 4 lbs 13 ozs.

The White-Fish lives in the lakes of the Baltic Sea coast, in Poland, the USSR, Finland, Sweden, Norway and as far west as Denmark and North Germany, occurring also in the Upper Volga basin (Valdai Hills).

The flavour of its flesh is excellent. Its mass occurrence makes it important for fresh water fisheries, being suitable for breeding in lakes and clean reservoirs.

(H.)

Coregonus albula

The Lavaret

Coregonus lavaretus maraena (BLOCH, 1779)

The Lavaret is one of the most important species of the genus *Coregonus*. It is an extraordinarily variable species whose forms used to be considered as separate species. Today we rank them all in one species, their differentiation being very difficult. One of the most popular is the Lavaret — *Coregonus lavaretus maraena*.

The body shape and general appearance are reminiscent of the cyprinoid *Vimba*. The body is covered with medium-sized easily detachable scales. The head is relatively small, with a ventral protrusible mouth. The fins are strong, and the caudal fin is forked. The dorsal fin has 2—4 hard rays and 9—11 soft rays, the anal fin 3 or 4 hard and 10—12 soft rays. The lateral line has 95—100 scales; the first branchial arch has 27—37 long gill rakers. The back is dark green or dark blue in colour with silvery white flanks and belly.

One of the most important prerequisites for the breeding of the Lavaret is pure, cold water with a sufficiently high oxygen content. The characteristic habitat of the Lavaret is a glacial lake of a depth of 350 ft or more. The fish live mostly on the bottom, rising to the surface only during the spawning season, i.e. in November and December. In ponds, where its breeding is artificial, it must be spawned artificially. The sign of maturity is the presence of the so called "nuptial tubercles" in the centre of its scales which occur in both males and females in continuous rows above or even below the lateral line. The Lavaret attains a length of 24—28 ins and a weight of 10 lbs or over, in ponds up to 14 lbs. Particularly large specimens can reach a weight of 20 lbs and a length of $4\frac{1}{2}$ ft. The food consists of plankton and benthos, larger specimens feeding also on fish.

The Lavaret lives in deep lakes of North Germany, particularly in Pomerania, from where it has been exported to other localities during the last century. It is often kept in fishponds (e.g. in Czechoslovakia), and recently in artificial reservoirs.

The economic importance of the Lavaret and the White-Fish is considerable. They occur in considerable numbers, forming the most valuable components of the ichthyo-fauna of some regions. They are appreciated for their fine, white flesh with characteristic smell and taste. Smoked Lavaret is considered a delicacy.

(H.)

Coregonus lavaretus maraena

The Houting

Coregonus lavaretus oxyrhynchus LINNAEUS, 1758

One of the migratory species of the White-Fish family of the North Sea and the Atlantic is the Houting — *Coregonus lavaretus oxyrhynchus*, well known on the coasts of France, Holland, Belgium, Germany, Denmark and other Scandinavian countries.

The shape of its body suggests a carp or herring-like fish. A characteristic feature is the head, which protrudes into a conical soft greyish-blue to black snout below which there is a narrow mouth considerably shifted to the rear. Its dorsal fin has 3 or 4 hard and 9—13 soft rays, the anal fin 3 or 4 hard and 11—14 soft rays. The lateral line comprises 84 to 100 scales, and the first branchial arch bears 25 to 44 gill rakers. The greyish blue, green or bluish-green colour of its back changes into a lighter yellowish white colour with silvery lustre in its flanks and belly. In the spawning season the males and females develop the characteristic nuptial tubercles showing in the form of sharp conical growths on the scales. These cones are continuous in two rows above and 3 rows below the lateral line.

The Houting is a migratory marine fish, entering rivers and large lakes only in the spawning season. Its ascent to the spawning places begins at the end of summer and the beginning of autumn. Spawning begins in October or November, proceeding during mild weather long into December. The female lays 20—40, sometimes even 50 thousand eggs. After hatching the young immediately set off downstream to the sea. They feed chiefly on worms and molluscs; they probably dig these out of the sea bed by means of their prolonged snout, which may be as much as 16 ins long.

The Houting lives in North Sea and in the western part of the Baltic Sea. For spawning it ascends the Rhine, the Weser, the Elbe, and other rivers of south-west Europe as well as the lakes of southern Sweden, its habitat extending westwards, sometimes even as far as the British Isles. *Coregonus lavaretus* in general lives in the Atlantic Ocean, the North and Baltic Seas, in the rivers of Siberia and in the Baikal Sea. It is important particularly as a species of mass occurence, easily captured particularly during its ascent to the spawning places. It has very palatable flesh, but is of no interest to anglers.

(H.)

52

Coregonus lavaretus oxyrhynchus

The Grayling

Thymallus thymallus (LINNAEUS, 1758)

The Grayling, an exquisite inhabitant of streams and brooks below the mountains, is particularly popular with anglers specializing in fly-fishing, a pursuit affording unforgettable memories. The Grayling is a representative of another branch of the salmonid fishes the genus *Thymallus* forming a transition between the Salmon, Trout and Char on the one hand and the White-Fish on the other hand.

The characteristic feature of the Grayling is its large dorsal fin, in which it differs conspicuously from other freshwater fishes. The caudal fin is forked. The scales are large, firmly embedded in the skin, mounted on the body so as to form a regular hexagonal pattern. The number of scales in the lateral line varies between 74 and 96. The dorsal fin has 4—7 hard and 13—17 soft rays, the anal fin 2—4 hard and 8—11 soft rays. The first branchial arch numbers 21—29 gill rakers. The maxillary teeth are very small and weak and hardly perceptible. The colouring of the Grayling varies a great deal. In northern Europe it is generally darker, in other countries it is of a lighter green or golden hue with a great number of black spots on the back and flanks. The dorsal fin has chessboard markings, its rear part — particularly in males — being extended into a characteristic pendant shape.

The Grayling is a non-migratory salmonid fish characteristic of the rivers below the mountains. It spawns early in the spring, one female laying 2 to 36 thousand eggs on the stony or gravelly river bed. The staple food of the Grayling consists of air and water insects, larger specimens also feeding on small fish. It may reach a length of 18 ins and a weight of 3 lbs although it more frequently grows to only $1\frac{1}{2}$ lbs. Probably the biggest Grayling ever caught came from the river Wyly in England (1883); it weighed 4 lbs 9 ozs.

The habitat of the Grayling covers the whole of Europe except for the South of France and Spain. During the spawning season it ascends as high as 6000 ft above sea level. Related species are found in Asia and North America.

The Grayling is particularly appreciated by anglers, who enjoy its fly-fishing. In some regions, particularly in the north, it is also caught in nets. Its flesh has a distinctive thymy flavour.

(H.)

Thymallus thymallus

The Common Pike

Esox lucius LINNAEUS, 1758

The very ancient family *Esocidae* includes only one genus and six species living in the Nothern hemisphere. Europe is the habitat of one species only, *Esox lucius*, the Common Pike.

The whole appearance of the Pike betrays its predatory character. The head is long and compressed, the mouth wide and deeply cleft, provided with long, hooked teeth fused with the bone. Its eyes are situated high on both sides of the head and are protected by marked sockets. The Pike attains a length of $3\frac{1}{2}$—5 ft and a weight of 60 lbs. However, Pike up to $3\frac{1}{2}$ ft long and 16—24 lbs in weight are usually encountered. The dorsal fin has 6—10 hard and 13—16 soft rays, the pectoral fins 1 hard and 12—16 soft rays, the anal fin 4—5 hard and 10—13 soft rays. In the lateral line there are 121—144 scales, above it 14—17, below it 12—15 scales, the lateral line itself covering several rows of scales.

The Pike seeks slow-running water with numerous bends and secondary branches. It thrives also in still water and closed reservoirs. When young it feeds on plankton and small benthos. As soon as it has attained a length of 2 ins, however, it becomes carnivorous. At first it feeds on small fish, later finding more bulky food in the form of bigger fish and other vertebrates. With sufficient food young Pike grow very quickly, attaining a length of 16—20 ins and a weight of 2—6 lbs in their third year. Maturing begins in the second or third year. It spawns very early in the spring, after the thaw (in March and April). For the purpose of spawning the Pike leaves its usual haunts and seeks shallow water, such as freshly flooded meadows. The number of eggs depends on the size of the fish, varying between 10 and 400 thousand. The eggs are 2.5 mm in diameter. The development of the eggs takes 120—150 degree-days (e.g. 12—15 days at a temperature of 10° C).

The Pike is found throughout Europe with the exception of the Iberian Peninsula, South Italy, Dalmatia, and the Yugoslav part of the Balkan Peninsula. In Asia it occurs in the rivers emptying into the Aral Sea and the Arctic Ocean, in North America from Alaska to New York and Ohio.

Pike is a valuable fish both from the economic and from the angling point of view. It is successfully caught by live baiting, spinning or trolling.

(H.)

Esox lucius

The Roach

Rutilus rutilus (LINNAEUS, 1758)

The Roach is the most common fish of lowland waters with very frequent occurrence, representing the Carp family *(Cyprinidae)* which comprises some 200 species. Its mouth has no teeth, and the fifth pair of branchial arches are modified as pharyngeal teeth. The shape, number, and the rows of these pharyngeal teeth are reliable characteristics in distinguishing individual Cyprinid species.

The body is slender and elongated, laterally compressed, with arched back and centrally situated mouth. The pharyngeal teeth are flattened at the ends and arranged in a single row. A characteristic feature is the red iris of the eye. The scales are conspicuous, rather large, and arranged in regular rows. Another typical feature of the Roach is the colouring of the fins. The caudal and dorsal fins are grey with red background, all other fins being orange red. The dorsal fin has 3 hard and 9—11 soft rays, the pectoral fins 1 hard and 15 soft rays, the ventral 1 or 2 hard and 8 soft rays, and the anal fin 3 hard and 9—11 soft rays. The caudal fin has 19 soft rays. The lateral line comprises 38—49 scales.

The Roach is very widespread, occurring frequently even in trout streams. It prefers slowly flowing waters with a soft river bed. It spawns in April and May in shallow overgrown waters; a female weighing 2 lbs lays as many as 100 thousand eggs. In the third year the Roach attains a length of 4—6 ins. It has been known to live to an age of 18 years but, as a rule, only lives for 8—10 years.

In the spawning season the male develops nuptial tubercles on the head and flanks.

The Roach occurs all over Europe east of the Pyrenees and north of the Alps.

In some countries the economic importance of the Roach is not fully appreciated. In countries with a highly developed fishing industry it is caught for industrial purposes and is even canned.

It is very popular with anglers and can be caught on the rod all the year round. It also forms an important part of the diet of predatory fish.

The Roach is very successfully caught on the rod with light or medium weight tackle, using a caterpillar, pastry or potato as bait.

(H.)

Rutilus rutilus — male

The Chub

Leuciscus cephalus (LINNAEUS, 1758)

The Chub is the best known and most widespread member of the carp family *(Cyprinidae)*, often confused with its close relations, such as *Leuciscus leuciscus* (the Dace) and *Leuciscus idus* (the Silver Orfe).

The head of the Chub is large and wide, with a wide terminal mouth provided with thick lips, these characteristics distinguishing it from related species.

The body of the Chub is cylindrical and elongated, covered with characteristic large, well adhering black-edged scales. The pectoral fins are greyish or colourless, the ventral and anal fins reddish, the dorsal and the wide caudal fins greyish green with slight reddish tinge. The large eyes have a golden iris. The flanks are silvery, the belly white (or yellowish in old specimens). In trout-inhabited waters the Chub has very fine coloration, its gill covers being sometimes of a yellowish or golden hue. The anal fin has 3 hard and 9 or 10 soft rays; its corners are rounded and its lower edge convex. The dorsal fin has 3 hard and 8 or 9 soft rays, the pectoral fin has 1 hard and 16 or 17 soft rays. The lateral line comprises 44—46 scales, with 8 or 9 rows of scales above and 4 or 5 rows below it.

The Chub lives in clean, slowly flowing waters, but adjusts itself well to life in still water and reservoirs. It stays mostly in the upper layers of water, and is also often found below sluices where food is plentiful.

In running water the Chub ascends even very high into trout streams where, however, its presence is undesirable. It is very cautious and shy, particularly when older. When in danger it seeks shelter below scoured river banks or under stones.

It does not grow too quickly. In the first year it attains a length of 2—3 ins, in the second 4—5 ins, in the third 6—9 ins, its weight amounting, on the average, to 8 lbs, rarely 12—14 lbs or — in Eastern Europe — as much as 16 lbs.

Leuciscus cephalus — river form

The Chub - *continued*

It has very good reproductive capacity, spawning from April to the end of June. Prior to spawning the nuptial tubercles appear on the heads of the males whose fins also glow red. The female lays 50,000—100,000 eggs of 1.5 mm diameter on water plants, stones or even floating branches. During the spawning season the Chub often ascends high into shallow brooks. The males mature at the end of their second year, the females at the end of the third year when they weigh 3—6 ozs.

The food of the Chub consists of water plants and insects that have fallen into the water, larvae of aquatic insects, worms, and molluscs. Very old specimens feed on small fish and crayfish. It is very voracious.

The Chub occurs in European rivers — in England, southern Scotland, north and north-west France, Germany, Poland, south Norway, south Sweden and south Finland, being absent from Ireland, Denmark and the river Pechora.

Because of its good reproductive ability it forms valuable food for predatory fishes. In trout-inhabited waters it not only devours the young salmonid fish and their eggs, but also successfully competes with them for food. Being a cautious and shy fish, it is very popular among anglers. However, very fine tackle has to be used to deceive it. In the rivers below the mountains the Chub can be successfully caught on artificial fly or even live insects; in summer cherries are used as bait. For hand or float fishing peas are very popular, while in turgid water it can often be caught on a worm. The most exciting method which can be employed in any season, however, is spinning.

The flesh of the Chub is not particularly valuable, especially in summer and in the lowlands, because of its softness. Chub caught in clean, running water, however, are quite palatable.

(M.)

Leuciscus cephalus — lake form

The Silver Orfe

Leuciscus idus (LINNAEUS, 1758)

The Orfe occurs very frequently in the lower parts of large rivers, its refinement, in which it differs from other species of the family *Cyprinidae*, making it valuable for angling. One of its varieties, the red coloured Golden Orfe, is often kept in park lakes and ponds. In its mode of life it does not differ from the silvery species.

The body shape of the Silver Orfe is transitional between the Chub and the Dace. It has a small, blunt head with an obliquely cleft mouth and small but distinct scales arranged in regular rows. The lateral line runs parallel with the belly line. The dorsal fin has 3 hard and 8 or 9 soft rays, the pectoral fin one hard and 15 or 16 soft rays, the abdominal fin 3 hard and 8 soft rays, the distinctly concave anal fin having 3 hard and 9—11 soft rays. The forked caudal fin includes 19 soft rays. The lateral line comprises 56—61 scales. The basic coloration is greyish-blue or blackish-blue, with silvery flanks and a white or greyish belly.

The Silver Orfe seeks large, deep, relatively clean waters where it is found in large numbers. The spawning season covers the months of April and May, when the Orfe congregates. An adult female may lay as many as 100 thousand eggs on fine roots of water weeds in overgrown areas or near the banks. The Orfe is rather a small fish, attaining, on an average, a weight of about 1 lb and a length of 12—16 ins. In Finland, for example, the Orfe lives for about 14 years. When young it feeds on plankton; older specimens seek large water fauna, thus competing with other fishes.

The Silver Orfe occurs from the Rhine to the Lena and from the Danube to the Don, Volga, Ural and Emba, also being found in Siberian rivers. Because of its cautiousness and cunning it is very popular with anglers. It can be successfully caught by float fishing, but artificial fly fishing is particularly exciting. In the lower reaches of rivers where it occurs in large numbers it is also of some industrial importance.

(M.)

Leuciscus idus

The Schneider

Alburnoides bipunctatus (BLOCH, 1783)

The coloration of the Schneider is not nearly so varied as that of the Minnow. It is dark, inconspicuous, often with spots above the lateral line, which comprises 44—51 scales bordered with a double discontinued band. Another dark band extends along the centre of the body. The belly is light, greyish to silvery white.

The habitat of the Schneider is identical to that of the Minnow. The spawning season covers the months of April and May, when the eggs are laid on stones or gravel. The food of the Schneider consists of small aquatic fauna, and even eggs of other fishes. Adult specimens grow to a length of 4 ins, never more than 6 ins.

The Schneider is found in almost all of Europe with the exception of Ireland, England, Denmark, Sweden and Finland, and the countries to the South of the Alps. It has no direct economic importance. It is often used in bait fishing for predatory fishes.

(H.)

The Minnow

Phoxinus phoxinus (LINNAEUS, 1758)

The Minnow is a small cyprinid fish typical of clean mountain waters which it inhabits in association with the Trout, Bullhead, Schneider and Stone Loach.

It has a slender, elongate body with a relatively long caudal peduncle and a fairly large head. Its dorsal fin has 3 hard and 7 soft rays, the anal fin 3 hard and 6 or 7 soft rays. The body is covered with small scales, the lateral line numbering 80—92 of them. The semi-ventral crescent-shaped mouth is small. The coloration of the Minnow is very diverse, the basic colour being green, yellowish or gold; the belly is white or yellowish, the belly of the males in the spawning season being orange or red. The flanks are covered with dark spots. In the spawning season the males may be almost black, and the corners of their mouths are sometimes crimson; on their heads there are often relatively large nuptial tubercles.

Spawning takes place in the spring, through April to July. The females lay their eggs on sand or stones. The Minnow feeds on plankton, benthos, and on insects which have fallen into the water. It lives for 3 to 5 years, attaining a length of 3 or 4 ins, rarely 5 ins.

The Minnow lives in almost all rivers and brooks of Europe, occuring in considerable numbers in suitable localities. It has no industrial importance. In brooks, however, it often represents the only food of large trout.

(H.)

Alburnoides bipunctatus

Phoxinus phoxinus — male and female in spawning season

The Rudd

Scardinius erythrophthalmus (LINNAEUS, 1758)

The Rudd is a common cyprinid fish very similar to the Roach, important because it feeds chiefly on vegetable food.

It can easily be distinguished from the Roach by the position of its dorsal fin which is shifted well towards the tail. The central mouth of the Rudd slants sharply upwards. There is a conspicuous difference in the iris of the two species, which is yellowish to orange in the Rudd and crimson in the Roach. The pharyngeal teeth are arranged in two rows. The front row usually has 5 large teeth on each bone, the second row as a rule has 3. The coloration of the Rudd is more variegated than that of the Roach. The pectoral and caudal fins are more or less scarlet, the dorsal fin grey. The belly of the Rudd is keeled, while that of the Roach is rounded. The whole body of the Rudd is higher and shorter than that of the Roach. Large, distinct scales are arranged in regular rows. The dorsal fin has 2 or 3 hard and 8 or 9 soft rays, the anal fin 3 hard and 9—12 soft rays. The lateral line comprises 38—42 scales.

The Rudd occurs in large numbers particularly in the lower reaches of rivers. Its mode of life is similar to that of the Roach. It is often found in neglected, overgrown creeks, and does not frequent the swift-flowing rivers where the Roach is found, tending to stay near the banks and at the bottom.

The spawning season covers the months of April and May. The female lays some 80—100 thousand reddish eggs on delicate water plants. The eggs are 1 mm in diameter, and develop in 7—14 days.

The young feed mostly on zooplankton. When they are about 3 ins long, they begin to feed on plants. The food of adult specimens consists of soft water plants and filamentous algae, a diet frequently supplemented with insects that have fallen into the water. In its first year the Rudd attains a length of 2—3 ins, in the second year 3—4 ins. On an average, adult specimens grow to a length of 10—12 ins, when they weigh 10—14 ozs, the maximum weight may be as much as 4 lbs.

The Rudd is found throughout Europe with the exception of Greece, the Iberian Peninsula and northern Scandinavia.

It can be caught by fly-fishing, hand or float fishing. It forms a staple food of predatory game fish.

(M.)

Scardinius erythrophthalmus

The Rapfen

Aspius aspius (LINNAEUS, 1758)

The Rapfen is one of the most beautiful and most elegant of cyprinid fishes, differing from the other members of this family in the slender, torpedo-shaped body which reveals its predatory character.

The body is elongated, moderately compressed, with slightly curved belly and pointed head. The wide, cleft mouth is provided with strong lips. Smallish scales are arranged in regular rows and have a bluish-silvery lustre, particularly in Summer. The pectoral, dorsal, and anal fins are all sharply pointed.

The concave dorsal fin has 3 hard and 8 soft rays, the anal fin 2 or 3 hard and 12—14 soft rays. The lateral line comprises 65—70 scales. As in other cyprinids the coloration of the Rapfen is simple, varying from dark grey to greyish green. The belly is silvery, the pectoral and ventral fins pale grey with a distinct reddish tinge, particularly in the spawning season.

The Rapfen lives in large rivers, or still waters and backwaters, where it floats near the surface, feeding on small fish. Its presence is often betrayed by noisy echoes.

It spawns in May and June in clean running water. The female lays 80 to 200 thousand eggs, 1.6 mm in diameter, on stones. Their development takes about 6 days, the exact period depending on the temperature of water. The young feed on small animals, particularly larvae and worms. Older specimens feed mostly on small fishes. The growth of the Rapfen is very rapid; the fish attains, on the average, a length of 2 ft and a weight of 4—8 lbs. Specimens over 3 ft long weighing as much as 30 lbs, which are caught now and then, however, are fairly rare.

The Rapfen is found in rivers emptying into the Northern, Baltic, Black and Caspian Seas. It is not found in France, Great Britain, Denmark, Switzerland, the Iberian Peninsula, Italy, the southern part of the Balkan Peninsula, or the rivers emptying into the Arctic Ocean.

Due to its relatively infrequent occurrence it is of little economic importance. From the angler's point of view, however, the Rapfen is a valuable fish, chiefly because of its size, mistrust, and cunning.

(M.)

Aspius aspius

The Tench

Tinca tinca (LINNAEUS, 1758)

The Tench is the best known cyprinid fish second only to the carp itself. The shape and coloration of its body are so characteristic that it is impossible to mistake it for any other member of the carp family.

The body of the Tench is short and relatively high, its cross section oval. The dorsal line rises slowly from the head towards the dorsal fin, the belly line being almost straight. The tapered head is provided with a small, partly protrusible mouth with a pair of short barbels on its upper lip. The scales are very small, hardly visible. The dorsal fin is very high, arched, and has 3 or 4 hard and 8 or 9 soft rays, the large caudal fin is squarely truncated. The lateral line comprises 87—115 scales. Prior to sexual maturity the second ray of the ventral fin of the male grows considerably, and the fins become stronger and larger, reaching as far as the anal orifice; in the females they remain short and weak.

The Tench inhabits still or slow-running water. It stays at the bottom, seeking food. Tench retreat to the deepest places for the winter, like the Carp does, remaining immobile until the advent of spring, as they require little oxygen. Spawning is from April to July, in shallow, overgrown places where the female lays 100 to 200 thousand eggs 1.5 mm in diameter. The development of the eggs takes 4—8 days, a twelve-day embryo measuring $\frac{1}{2}$ in in length. The food of the Tench is similar to that of other cyprinid fishes, consisting of small plankton at first, and later of insect larvae, worms, crustaceans and molluscs. The Tench can reach a maximum weight of 15 lbs, usually, however, growing to only 4 lbs. In its first year it attains an average length of 6 ins, in the second year 9 ins, and in the third 10 ins.

The Tench is found throughout Europe, Siberia, and the Caucasus. It does not occur in the rivers emptying into the Arctic Ocean, Norway, Sweden, Finland, Dalmatia or Crimea.

Because of its tasty, fat flesh it is very much sought after on the market, also forming an important supplementary fish of carp ponds. It is very popular with anglers, too, particularly the bigger specimens.

(M.)

Tinca tinca

The Dace

Leuciscus leuciscus (LINNAEUS, 1758)

The Dace is typical of the middle reaches of rivers and brooks, occurring occasionally in lakes and reservoirs.

Its elongate, cylindrical body is provided with a relatively large head. The dorsal fin has 3 hard and 7 or 8 soft rays, the anal fin 3 hard and 7—9 soft rays. The lateral line comprises 45—55 scales. It differs from the related and very similar Chub in its concave anal fin.

The Dace is a freshwater fish, only rarely found in brackish waters. It usually lives in small shoals. It attains a maximum length of 12—14 ins and a weight of 1—1½ lbs.

Its habitat includes Northern and Central Europe with the exception of the Iberian, Italian and Balkan Peninsulas, Scotland, and Ireland.

It is rarely sought by professional fishermen, but highly appreciated by anglers as a cautious, shy fish requiring fine tackle and some skill.

(H.)

The Gudgeon

Gobio gobio (LINNAEUS, 1758)

The Gudgeon is a small cyprinid fish living in both still and running water.

Its elongated, spindle-shaped or cylindrical body has a long tail and a massive head. The dorsal fin has 3 hard and 7 soft rays, the anal fin 2 or 3 hard and 5—7 soft rays. The lateral line comprises 40—45 scales with 5 or 6 rows of scales above and 3 or 4 rows below it. At the corners of its mouth are a pair of barbels.

The Gudgeon is a shoaling freshwater fish also living, however, in the brackish or slightly salty water of the Gulf of Finland and the Baltic. It can grow to a maximum length of 10 ins and a weight of 10—11 ozs, attaining as a rule, however, a length of only 4—6 ins.

It is found in the whole of Europe with the exception of Norway, northern Sweden and Finland, Scotland, Greece, southern and central Italy and Spain.

It is a favourite with anglers, particularly in western Europe, its fishing, however, requires very fine tackle and angling technique.

(H.)

74

Leuciscus leuciscus

Gobio gobio

The Näsling (The Broad-Snout)

Chondrostoma nasus (LINNAEUS, 1758)

The Näsling is one of the few European fishes to feed mostly on plants even when mature, and probably the only species living largely on algae; it is well adapted to this type of diet.

The Näsling is a very handsome fish with a slender body and a muscular tail capable of overcoming even the swift flow of the rivers in and below the mountains in which it lives. Its dorsal fin has 3 or 4 hard and 9 or 10 soft rays, the anal fin 3 hard and 9—12 soft rays. The lateral line is mildly deflected and contains 56—63 scales. In general appearance the Näsling resembles the *Vimba*, even in the position of its mouth, which is situated below a wide and broad snout. It differs from it, however, in having a smaller number of rays in the anal fin and particularly in the shape of the mouth. While the mouth of the *Vimba* is horseshoe-shaped, that of the Näsling has the appearance of a straight transverse slit. The sharp-edged lips are horny and serve the Näsling for scraping algae and other organisms from stones. In the spawning season several rows of sharp cones — the nuptial tubercles — appear on the back of the males. In addition to this their coloration becomes more vividly blue or dark mauve.

The Näsling is a gregarious fish, forming large shoals in swift, clean mountain rivers, and also in the still waters of lakes and reservoirs containing clean, cool water with abundant oxygen and food. It spawns in the spring, throughout April and the beginning of May. In the spawning season large shoals of Näsling ascend the rivers, where they lay their eggs in running water on the clean stones or gravel.

The Näsling feeds on lower plants and organisms adhering to stones which it grazes by means of the sharp edge of its lower jaw, leaving characteristic traces in the form of wide scratches. It grows to a length of 10—14 ins and a weight of $4\frac{1}{2}$ lbs.

Its habitat is Central Europe, the rivers emptying into the Northern and the Baltic Seas, and the Danube basin. It does not occur in the Elbe basin. Related species and forms live in eastern Europe and in Asia Minor.

In the countries of its mass occurrence it is very valuable for industrial purposes. It is also very popular with anglers and can be caught with fine tackle.

(H.)

Chondrostoma nasus

The Bitterling

Rhodeus sericeus amarus (BLOCH, 1782)

The small Bitterling is a fish of no economic importance. Nevertheless its interesting breeding habits make it worth including in this book.

In general appearance it resembles a small Crucian Carp. However, it is lustrous, with a steel-blue shining band on the caudal peduncle, and has no more than 4—7 scales in its lateral line. In the spawning season the male has nuptial tubercles on its snout and above its eyes, its coloration becoming intensely blue or mauve. The urogenital papilla of the female is protracted into the form of an ovipositor, often longer than the fish itself.

By means of this ovipositor the female Bitterling lays its eggs in the mantle cavity of a living mussel where the eggs are well protected from their enemies and can slowly develop. After hatching, which takes about 3—4 weeks, the young Bitterling remain with their host for some time, leaving it, when they are capable of leading an independent life, directly through the inhalant siphon. The Bitterling feeds on small plankton and detritus, living only 3 to 4, or at the most 5 years. It attains a maximum length of $2\frac{3}{4}$ ins and a weight of 5 or 6 grams. It is found throughout Europe as far as the Ural Mountains, with the exception of Italy, Spain, England, Ireland, Denmark and Scandinavia.

(H.)

The Bleak

Alburnus alburnus (LINNAEUS, 1758)

The Bleak is a slender fish living in both still and moving water, often appearing even in trout-inhabited zones at higher altitudes.

Its dorsal fin has 3 or 4 hard and 7—9 soft rays, the anal fin 3 hard and 15—19 soft rays. The lateral line comprises 42—52 scales. The mouth is turned upwards, eyes large, scales silvery.

The Bleak spawns in the spring (April and May) depositing its eggs on water plants, and sometimes on stones. It feeds on plankton, particularly zooplankton, and insects which have fallen into the water. It lives for 6 years at the most, attaining a length of 6—8 ins and a weight of up to 1 oz.

It is found throughout Europe with the exception of Scotland and Ireland.

Because of its mass occurrence it is important to the canning industry. From its scales "Essence d'Orient" (pearl essence) is made, which is used in the production of artificial pearls. It is often sought by anglers, requiring, however, the finest tackle.

(H.)

Rhodeus sericeus — male and female in spawning season

Alburnus alburnus

The Barbel

Barbus barbus (LINNAEUS, 1758)

The Barbel is a very widespread and well-known cyprinid fish characteristic of the swiftly flowing middle reaches of rivers which in the past used actually to be known as barbel zones.

It has a slim, elongated body of more or less circular cross section, with a slightly compressed belly, excellently adapted to life in swiftly running water and at the bottom of rivers. The medium sized scales are deeply embedded in the skin and arranged in regular rows. Its brown eyes, situated high on the head, are relatively small. The ventral mouth, provided with fleshy lips and two pairs of barbels, is well adapted to searching for food in sand and under small stones. The colouring is inconspicuous, well matched to the colour of the river bed. The dorsal and anal fins are relatively short, the former having 3 or 4 hard and 8 or 9 soft rays, the latter 3 hard and 5 soft rays. The lateral line comprises 56—60 scales.

The Barbel lives in rivers with clean water, particularly in running water with a hard riverbed and plenty of shelter. It penetrates as far as the lower boundary of the trout zone and can be found even in the same waters as the Trout and Grayling. It leaves its shelter towards the evening to seek food in the swiftly flowing parts of the river. Its food consists mostly of larvae of insects, worms, molluscs and other small aquatic organisms, as well as water weeds; larger specimens even hunt smaller fish.

The Barbel spawns relatively late, at the end of May, in medium deep and not-too-swiftly flowing waters and in the rivers below the mountains as late as June or the beginning of July. The female lays only a few thousand eggs of 2 mm diameter which hatch in 6—8 days. The growth of the young fishes is fairly rapid. In the first year they weigh up to $\frac{1}{2}$ oz, in the second 4—5 ozs, in the third 20—21 ozs. Adult Barbel attain a maximum weight of 16—26 lbs and a length of 3 feet.

The Barbel in found in western and Central Europe with the exception of Ireland, Denmark, Scandinavia and the southern European peninsulas. There are several forms in the individual river basins.

The Barbel is very highly appreciated by anglers. In recent years its number has been rapidly decreasing due to excessive pollution of rivers. Its speedy growth and good utilization of food make it a fish of considerable economic importance.

When caught on the hook, it is very game. Successful baits include rainworms, the larvae of bank-bait, leeches or natural food. A struggle with a 13—20 lb Barbel can afford a great deal of excitement.

(M.)

Barbus barbus

The Silver Bream

Blicca bjoerkna (LINNAEUS, 1758)

Although resembling the Bream, the Silver Bream is classified as an independent genus — *Blicca* — of the family *Cyprinidae*.

It differs from the Bream in the number of rays in its anal fin (19—23 in the Silver Bream and 24—30 in the Bream) and the number of the scales in the lateral line (43—51 and 51—60 respectively). The dorsal fin is particularly high and sharply pointed, the caudal fin being deeply forked. The fins are reddish, the dorsal, anal and caudal fins being bluish grey. The hooked pharyngeal teeth are arranged in two rows. The conspicuously large eyes have a silvery iris. The dorsal fin has 3 hard and 8 or 9 soft rays.

The Silver Bream inhabits lowland waters, ponds and lakes. It lives in small shoals keeping close to the banks. It is very agile and voracious. It spawns in May and June in shallow, thickly vegetated water near the banks. At a water temperature of about 20°C, the female lays as many as 100 thousand eggs of 1.6—2 mm diameter on clumps of river weed. Hatching takes 4 days. The growth rate varies depending on available food, up to a weight of 1 lb and a length of 6—8 ins. Individual specimens 12—14 ins long are very rare. The young feed mostly on algae, whirligig beetles and daphnial, the predominant food of the adults being zooplankton.

The Silver Bream lives in lowland rivers of Europe and Asia, in western France and eastern England, in the Gulf of Finland, the Ladoga and Onega Lakes, in Denmark and Finland up to latitude 63°43' North, in the rivers emptying into the Black Sea, the North Sea and in the river Kura basin.

Its economic importance is not great. It is, however, highly popular with anglers, particularly in the lower parts of rivers and in reservoirs, where it occurs in large numbers. When abundant, it affords suitable food to predatory fishes. It is not as shy and cautious as the Bream, and can be caught on paste or on boiled small maize grains.

(M.)

Blicca bjoerkna

The Bream

Abramis brama LINNAEUS, 1758

The Bream is one of the most frequent cyprinid fishes of lowland rivers which, due to its abundance, used to be known as the bream zones.

The body of the Bream is strongly compressed, its height equalling about one third of its length (excluding caudal fin). The head is small, blunt, devoid of barbels. When young the Bream is often mistaken for the Silver Bream from which it differs by the position of its mouth (in the Bream the mouth is ventral, in the Silver Bream central). The pharyngeal teeth are arranged in one row, those of the Silver Bream being arranged in two rows. The species differ also in the colour of their fins. The dorsal fin has 3 hard and 9 soft rays, the anal fin 3 hard and 23—30 soft rays, as compared with the Silver Bream whose anal fin comprises 3 hard and 19—23 soft rays. The scales are relatively large and arranged in regular rows, the belly and the part of the body in front of the pectoral fins being bare. The lateral line comprises 51—60 scales.

The Bream lives in quiet parts of rivers, with a soft bed, mostly at the bottom, where it seeks its food. It is a gregarious, rather shy fish. It spawns in warm weather, usually at night, in May and at the beginning of June, a little earlier than the carp, in shallow waters along the river banks. In the spawning season the males have conspicuous nuptial tubercles particularly on their heads and backs, smaller tubercles appearing also on the fins. The eggs are small, 1.5—1.8 mm in diameter, one female laying 200—300 thousand. On an average the Bream attains a length of 12—16 ins and a weight of 2—4½ lbs. Exceptional specimens may grow to a maximum of 30 ins and 30—35 lbs. When young the Bream feeds mostly on plankton, later on seeking its food at the river bottom in the form of larvae, molluscs, and worms. In the evenings it feeds also on littoral fauna.

The Bream occurs all over Europe with the exception of the Southern peninsulas. In the Caspian and Aral Sea territories there are several varieties.

The Bream, particularly when older, is a valuable fish for anglers, being mostly caught on floating bait. Its fishing, however, requires very fine tackle. Its tasty fat flesh also makes it economically important.

(M.)

84

Abramis brama

The Blue Bream

Abramis ballerus (LINNAEUS, 1758)

The Blue Bream is a typical cyprinid fish particularly abundant in lower parts of large rivers, such as the Danube and the Volga, in whose territories it is of considerable economic importance.

In appearance it is similar to *Abramis sapa*, which differs from the former in its fat, convex snout and the position of its mouth.

The Blue Bream has a high, compressed body which is less arched than that of the Bream, with a pointed head. Its eyes are also larger. The pharyngeal teeth are arranged in one row. One of the most important characteristics is the number of rays in the anal fin. The Blue Bream has 3 hard and 35—44 soft rays in its anal fin, its caudal fin being deeply forked. The dorsal fin has 3 hard and 8 or 9 soft rays. The lateral line comprises 66—73 scales. The flanks of the Blue Bream are silvery, the back is dark blue, the median fins grey and the paired fins yellowish with dark ends.

The Blue Bream inhabits the lower parts of rivers. It spawns in April and May in shallow places overgrown with grass. The female lays 5—20 thousand eggs 1.3—1.5 mm in diameter on the stems or leaves of sedge. Hatching takes 12—13 days. The growth rate is slow and very variable, depending on fluctuations of the water level with consequent variations of food supply. After a year the young may be from $\frac{1}{2}$ in to $\frac{3}{4}$ in long, after two years $\frac{3}{4}$ to $1\frac{1}{4}$ ins. On an average the Blue Bream grows to a length of 12—14 ins, rarely up to 16 ins, and a weight of $1\frac{1}{2}$ lbs. Sexual maturity comes at the end of the fourth year, when the fish measures 6—8 ins. In contrast with other cyprinids it feeds exclusively on plankton all the year round.

The Blue Bream is a migratory fish ascending the rivers in whose estuaries it lives. Its range includes the rivers emptying into the North and the Baltic Seas, and the Black and Caspian Seas from the Danube to the Ural.

In places where it is not common the Blue Bream is of no special economic importance. As a cyprinid fish it is important particularly because it uses the food which is left almost intact by other economically important species. It is considered a delicacy in some regions and is very much sought after.

(M.)

Abramis ballerus

The Zährte

Vimba vimba (LINNAEUS, 1758)

The Zährte is a beautiful, agile fish living at the bottom of rivers as well as in the Baltic and North Seas.

It resembles the Näsling *(Chondrostoma nasus)* from which it can be distinguished by its sturdier, high body, relatively long anal fin, elongate snout and a mouth shaped like a horseshoe. The mouth has not the sharp-edged, horny lips, but is protrusible like that of carp, bream, and other cyprinids. The dorsal fin has 3 hard and 17—21 soft rays, and the lateral line comprises 56—64 scales. The body beyond the pectoral fins is keeled. The first branchial arch numbers 16—20 gill rakers. The back is greyish blue, sometimes greenish blue, the flanks silvery. The dorsal and caudal fins are grey, all other fins pale yellow or orange. In the spawning season the males develop characteristic nuptial tubercles on the heads and bodies.

The Zährte is a migratory fish which leaves the sea and enters the rivers ascending as far as the parts below the mountains to spawn. There are, however, forms (e.g. *Vimba vimba carinata* from the Danube basin) which do not return to the sea, remaining in the rivers throughout their lives, and ascending into higher positions only for spawning. One female lays about 30 thousand eggs on the clean stony bottom directly in the stream of the river. The Zährte reaches a length of 20 ins and a weight of 2 lbs.

Its habitat includes the network of rivers emptying into the North Sea, the territories adjoining the Kattegat (the Vänern and Göta Lakes), the rivers emptying into the Baltic Sea from the Vistula to the Neva, South Finland and South Sweden. In the rivers emptying into the Black and Azov Seas the sub-species *Vimba vimba carinata* is found, in the Balkan, the Caspian Sea system and Asia Minor there are other sub-species. The Zährte is a very adjustable species easily adapting to life in still waters of reservoirs, where it forms varieties with high bodies.

Because of its tasty flesh, usually processed by smoking or marinating, the Zährte is very much appreciated, its fishing is on the increase. It is popular with anglers, too, being caught by hand or float fishing with fine tackle.

(H.)

Vimba vimba

The Ziege

Pelecus cultratus LINNAEUS, 1758

Pelecus cultratus is an interesting cyprinid fish differing from the remaining species of the family *Cyprinidae* in the general structure of its body, and particularly the position of its mouth and of the lateral line.

The body has a conspicuous knife-like shape with an almost straight back, and an arched belly devoid of scales. The mouth is situated high and has no teeth. The pharyngeal teeth are arranged in two rows in the 2,5—5,2 pattern.

The lateral line sinks steeply down to the belly, continuing in zig-zag direction along the flanks; it is easy to distinguish it from other cyprinid fishes on this characteristic. The body is covered with lustrous scales arranged in rows converging obliquely downwards. The eyes are relatively large. The pectoral fins are also conspicuous, being relatively long and narrow. The anal fin is long with the front rays longer than the rear ones, and has 3 hard and 24—29 soft rays. The dorsal fin is short and has 3 hard and 6—8 soft rays. The caudal fin is deeply forked. The lateral line comprises 90—115 scales, with 12—15 rows of scales above and 3—5 rows of scales below it. The coloration is similar to that of the Bleak. The scales are silvery, the back greenish blue, and the caudal and anal fins are the same colour as the body. The ventral and pectoral fins are almost colourless.

Pelecus cultratus lives in the sea. In the spawning season, in April and May, it ascends the rivers. One female lays 10—15 thousand eggs 1,3—1,5 mm in diameter which swell to 5—6 mm. After they have been deposited, the eggs float down the river, hatching in 7—8 days.

Its food consists of small water organisms and plankton, and later often small fishes.

The fish attains a length of 12—16 ins and a weight of 10—14 ozs. It grows to a length of 2 ft and a weight of 2 lbs at the most. It is mature in its third or fourth year.

Its range includes the Baltic, Black, Caspian and Aral Seas.

In the lower reaches of rivers it is of considerable industrial importance. Interest in it is also shown by anglers, as it can be easily caught by spinning.

(M.)

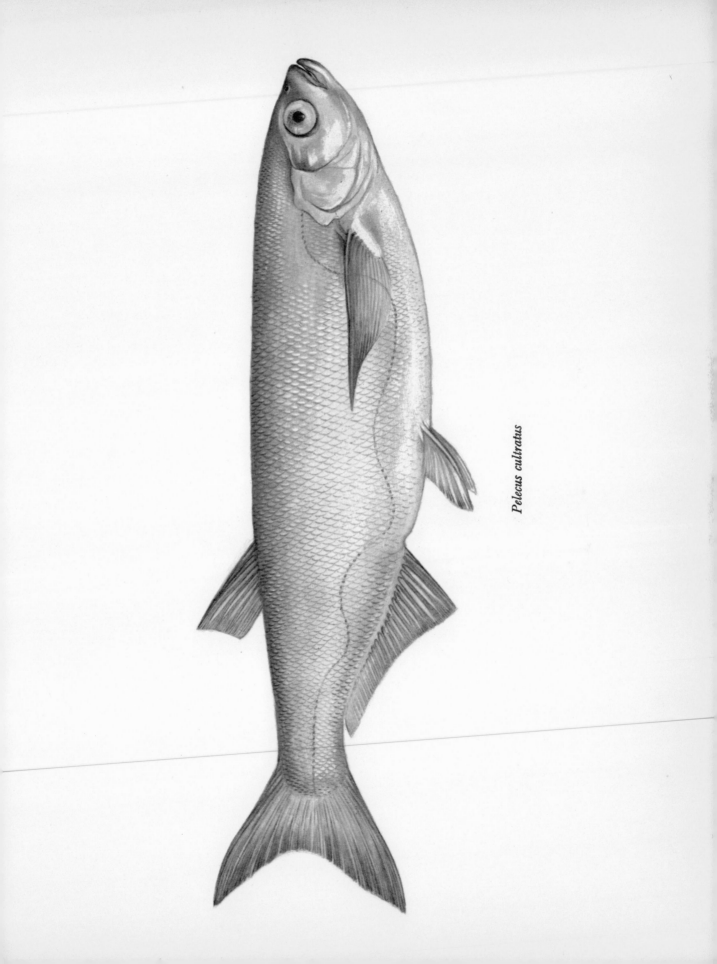

Pelecus cultratus

The Crucian Carp

Carassius carassius (LINNAEUS, 1758)

The Crucian Carp is a cyprinid fish less valuable, though closely related to the Common Carp, which it also resembles in appearance. Apart from other characteristics (e.g. the number of rays in the fins, the different number of pharyngeal bones and scales), the fundamental difference lies in the absence of barbels. As well as the common Crucian Carp various other species are known, e.g. *Carassius carassius morpha humilis*, *Carassius auratus auratus* (the Goldfish), *Carassius auratus gibelio* (the Prussian Carp), and others.

The dorsal line of the common Crucian Carp is arched, although the shape of the body is very variable and changes according to environment. In stagnant waters very deep-bodied specimens can be found, and in swiftly flowing waters with little food the body may be elongated. The head is relatively short and small, with a silvery iris to the eye. The gill covers are coarse to the touch. The pharyngeal teeth are arranged in one row according to the 4—4 pattern. On the first branchial arch there are 23—33 gill rakers. The lateral line comprises 28—33 scales. The long dorsal fin has 3 or 4 hard and 14—21 soft rays, the relatively short anal fin comprising 2 or 3 hard and 6—8 soft rays.

The Crucian Carp inhabits slow-moving lowland waters with numerous pools and secondary branches. It dwells mostly at the bottom, among the weeds, where it hunts for food. It has not high oxygen requirements and can live even in turbid or marshy waters. It spawns in shallow, overgrown places in May and June, one female laying 200—300 thousand eggs 1—2 mm in diameter on weeds. The Crucian Carp very easily interbreeds with the Common Carp; the resulting fishes grow more rapidly than the Crucian Carp. The food of the Crucian Carp consists chiefly of small aquatic fauna, particularly zooplankton. In its alimentary canal, however, larvae of various insects, e.g. dragon-flies, can also be found. Growth is slow, attaining a length of 14—20 ins and a maximum weight of 4 lbs.

Its range includes almost the whole of Europe from north-eastern France to Scandinavia, the littoral regions of the North, Black, and Caspian Seas, and the Arctic Ocean as far as the river Lena.

Its economic importance is negligible, and it does not interest anglers either. It is an unwelcome visitor in carp ponds as it successfully competes with other, more economically valuable fishes. It attains greater importance only in peaty regions with turbid waters.

(M.)

Carassius carassius

Carassius carassius m. *humilis*

The Common Carp

Cyprinus carpio LINNAEUS, 1758

Since time immemorial the Common Carp has ranked among the most popular fishes not only in Europe, but also on other continents, where it has been introduced. The original wild Common Carp occurs only in the Danube and in the river Tisa.

The shape of its body is always low and elongate, its home territory being the waters emptying into the Black, Caspian and Aral Seas and perhaps western Europe, the second centre being the territory of the Pacific coast from the Amur to Burma. It has also been introduced, for example, in Australia and New Zealand.

The Carp is an exquisite fish with a perfectly constructed muscular body, whose dorsal line forms a continuous curve. Considerable deviations can be found in various cultured varieties in which the back rises steeply beyond the head. The head is relatively small, asymmetrically tapered, with a small protrusible mouth provided with strong lips and four barbels. The mouth has no teeth and is capable of picking up even coarse food.

The carp has three rows of teeth arranged in the 1,1,3—3,1,1 pattern. Below them there is a callous pad which facilitates the crushing of food. The eyes are placed relatively high on the head. The gill covers are smooth, terminating in a leathery rim with which the carp can close its gill slits in adverse conditions (e.g. in mud). The external side of the first branchial arch bears 21—29 gill rakers. Regarding the internal organs, mention should be made of the simple alimentary canal which has no stomach and is surrounded by the long lobes of liver. In females the body cavity also contains the ovaries.

The fins of the Carp are regular and symmetrically distributed. The large dorsal fin has 3 or 4 hard and 18—20 soft rays, as a rule. The number of soft rays, however, can vary from 15—17 (rarely) to 21 or 22. The pectoral fins growing just below the gills have one hard and 15 or 16 soft rays. The ventral fins situated in about the middle of the length of the body have 2 hard and 8 or 9 soft rays. The trapezoidal anal fin has 3 hard and 5 soft

Cyprinus carpio — wild river species from the Danube

rays, the wide, forked caudal fin comprising 17—19 soft rays. The body of the original Common Carp is covered with scales arranged in regular rows and not very well grown into the skin. The lateral line has 30—40 scales, with 5 or 6 rows of scales above and 5 or 7 rows below it. The coloration of the Carp is rather variable, adaptable to various situations and the character of the bottom of the ponds where it lives.

The Carp is a thermophilic, gregarious fish dwelling mostly at the bottom of ponds. It thrives best in well warmed waters at lower elevations. It can adapt to coarser conditions which, however, impair its growth. According to the weather it does not only stay at the bottom, but sometimes rises to the surface where it basks on warm, sunny days. It is very shy and cautious. It attains sexual maturity in the third or fourth years, earlier in warmer climates.

The spawning season begins at the end of April and can extend to as late as June depending on the temperature of the water, which must be between 16 and 18°C. The female seeks shallow, overgrown places where she deposits the eggs, usually about 20 ins below water level. The eggs are 1.5 mm in diameter, their number depending on the weight of the fish, 50—100 thousand eggs being 1 lb of its weight. A female weighing 8 or 10 lbs can lay 600—900 thousand eggs. In water at 16°C the eggs hatch in 5 days. If the water temperature is higher, the hatching period is reduced to 3 days. The embryo, 5 or 6 mm long, feeds on its yolk sac for the first two or three days. The sac completely disappears after 8—10 days. After this period the young fishes feed on smaller plankton, particularly zooplankton. Later on they begin to eat larvae living at the bottom of shallow water, gradually including worms and insects in their diet. We can often also find fine algae in their alimentary canal. With a rise of water temperature also the intake of food increases, becoming greatest at a temperature of 17—25°C. As the water temperature is lowered,

Cyprinus carpio — Scale Carp

so the intake of food becomes lower. At a temperature of 2—5°C the carp takes no natural food at all, gathering at the bottom in selected places to hibernate. (The Carp has no demanding oxygen requirements. In winter 3 cm³ per litre of water is sufficient, in summer the requirement rises to a maximum of 3 or 4 to 7 cm³ of oxygen per litre.)

The growth of the Carp is very rapid, particularly in favourable habitats. In the first year the young reach a weight of ½ oz — 1 lb, in the second 5 ozs — 2 lbs, in the third 12 ozs — 4 lbs. In Java, with a mean annual temperature of 25—27°C, the Carp grows 3 to 5 times as quickly as in Central Europe. In Central European conditions the Carp achieves an average length of 20—24 ins and a weight of 4—10 lbs, the maximum being 40 ins and 40—65 lbs.

Its rapid growth, tasty flesh, good reproductive ability and modest requirements have led to the Carp's becoming the staple fish of warm water fisheries. This process began in the 15th—16th century when the Carp was domesticated and various pond forms were developed which can be identified according to their squamation. We distinguish four basic forms, the Scale Carp, the Mirror Carp, the Band Carp and the Leather Carp.

THE SCALE CARP differs from the original Common Carp by the whole shape of its body, which is elongate and of almost circular cross-section in the Common Carp. In the Scale Carp, on the other hand, living in good conditions with ample food, the dorsal line rises steeply beyond the head which is disproportionately small when compared with the height of its body. The height to length ratio of the river form is 1:3.2, that of the pond form being 1:2.8. The body of both forms is covered with scales arranged in regular rows extending from the head to the caudal fin. In river forms these rows can be interrupted or displaced in various ways, and individual scales can be larger than others. The lateral line, which is very conspicuous, may be irregular due to the irregularities of the scales. As a rule these phenomena result from interbreeding of the Scale Carp with the Mirror Carp or the Leather Carp.

Cyprinus carpio — Mirror Carp

The Common Carp - *continued*

The body of THE MIRROR CARP is not covered with scales all over, the scales covering only some of its parts in irregular patterns or individually. The scales are situated near the head and tail or on the back, rarely along the lateral line. If any scales are present along the lateral line, their arrangement is irregular, and their number does not exceed 36. The dorsal fin has 18—20 soft rays.

THE BAND CARP can easily be distinguished from the Mirror Carp by the fact that its scales are arranged in rows, one of which proceeds along the lateral line; its scales (not more than 40) differ from each other in both shape and size. Another row of scales follows the dorsal line and can have various irregularities. The characteristic distinguishing this form from others is the number of rays in the dorsal fin, which is 12—20.

THE LEATHER CARP is entirely devoid of scales. Exceptionally, individual scales can appear either in one row below the dorsal part of the body or near the caudal or other fins. The Leather Carp can easily be distinguished from the other forms by the number of soft rays in its dorsal (5—20) and ventral (6—8) fins. The lateral line is replaced by a narrow furrow.

The various kinds of squamation are due to various characteristics of the carp. Thus the Scale Carp lives at higher altitudes and in rougher conditions, while the Leather Carp and the Mirror Carp live at lower altitudes where they also grow more quickly. Growth is naturally influenced by food supply.

From the economic point of view the Carp is one of the most valuable fishes of the lower reaches of rivers and the most important fish of fish ponds. It surpasses all other fishes in breeding ability, resistance to disease, and the high quality of its flesh; these characteristics, as well as its cleverness, adroitness and gameness on the hook also make it very popular among anglers.

(M.)

Cyprinus carpio — Leather Carp

The Stone Loach

Noemacheilus barbatulus LINNAEUS, 1758

The Stone Loach looks somewhat like a small Weatherfish, without its conspicuous color-ation, however. Its elongated, spindle-shaped body is brown or brownish yellow with distinct darker marbling or blotches. The head is compressed from above, and the ventral mouth is provided with 2 pairs of rostral barbels and 1 pair of barbels growing from the corners. The dorsal fin has 3 or 4 hard and 7 soft rays, the anal fin 3 or 4 hard and 5 soft rays. Another characteristic feature is the truncated caudal fin. The tiny, almost imper-ceptible scales are arranged so that they do not overlap, but lie next to one another.

The Stone Loach lives in still and running water, often ascending high into mountain streams. It spends most of its time hiding in various shelters. In the spawning season it does not lay all of its eggs at once, depositing them in two or three batches so that the spawning season is rather long. It feeds mostly on zoobenthos, lives for 5 to 6 years and reaches a length of 6 ins, rarely 7 ins.

Its range covers the whole of Europe with the exception of Norway and northern Sweden.

It is of no economic importance, being used only as a bait for predatory fishes. Some gourmets enjoy its tasty flesh.

(H.)

The Spined Loach

Cobitis taenia LINNAEUS, 1758

The Spined Loach is closely related to the Stone Loach, being similar in appearance and having a similar mode of life. It differs from it, however, in its very flat head. Below each eye it has an erectile spine which can prick sharply, if the fish is handled incautiously. The puncture, however, is harmless. The basic coloration is pale yellow, with 10—18 large spots on the flanks and a large number of smaller spots on the back. On the upperside of the root of the caudal fin there is a dark crescent-shaped patch.

Like the Stone Loach, the Spined Loach lives in concealed places, avoiding still water. It seeks sandy places in which it hides so that only its head and caudal fin are visible. It feeds on small creatures, attaining a length of 5 inches at the most. The eggs are laid on water plants.

Its range covers the whole of Europe with the exception of Ireland, Wales, Scotland, Norway and North Sweden.

It is of no economic importance, but is often kept in aquaria.

(H.)

Noemacheilus barbatulus

Cobitis taenia

The Weather-Fish (The Pond Loach)

Misgurnus fossilis (LINNAEUS, 1758)

The Weather-Fish is the biggest representative of the Loach family *(Cobitidae)* and the only one to have any economic importance.

It has an elongated, low, laterally compressed body with a blunt head with five pairs of barbels; 2 pairs on the upper jaw at the end of the snout, another pair in the corners of the mouth, the remaining two pairs growing from the lower lip. The dorsal fin has 3 or 4 hard and 5—7 soft rays, the anal fin 3—5 hard and 5 or 6 soft rays. The basic yellowish brown colour is supplemented with distinct dark longitudinal stripes.

The Weather-Fish lives in the lowlands, preferring static water in overgrown river branches, creeks and marshes, i.e. quiet, still water with a muddy bottom in which it often burrows. It can even live in water with a low oxygen content, being equipped with so-called intestinal respiration. This often betrays its presence as it comes to the surface noisily swallowing air.

The Weather-Fish spawns in the Spring — April and May, sometimes even later. The female lays its eggs in batches, two or three times a year, some 150 thousand eggs altogether. The eggs are attached to water plants. After hatching the young retain the so-called external (larval) gills for some time in the form of filiform structures outside the head. The Weather-Fish feeds on molluscs, worms and insect larvae, reaching a length of 14 inches or more.

Its range includes the whole of Europe from France to the Ladoga Sea. It is absent, however, from the British Isles, Scandinavia, the Iberian and Italian peninsulas and Greece.

In territories where it is abundant the Weather-Fish is of local economic importance. It is caught into baskets, bownets, sometimes even on hook. The anglers use it as bait for Catfish, Barbel, Chub, etc.

(H.)

Misgurnus fossilis

The Catfish (Wels, Waller)

Silurus glanis (LINNAEUS, 1758)

The Catfish is a typical predator of lowland waters attaining considerable dimensions. It is the only European representative of the varied family *Siluridae* which comprises some 120 genera and over 1,000 species mostly living in fresh water.

The Catfish has an elongated, entirely naked body with soft, slimy skin and a deeply cleft broad mouth. Both jaws have small teeth arranged in four or five rows. The most characteristic feature of the Catfish is its barbels, one pair on the upper jaw, which are mobile and very long, reaching to the base of pectoral fins, the other two pairs on the lower jaw being stationary, reinforced with a cartilaginous base, and much shorter. The dorsal fin is very small, devoid of any hard rays, containing only 3—5 soft rays. The anal fin has 77—92 soft rays. A very large air-bladder is conspicuous among the anatomical features.

The Catfish is a thermophilic predatory fish living in deep slow-running waters with soft bottom, its principal habitat being lowland waters. As a rule it spends the day lying in deep water emerging to hunt for food either at sunset or early in the morning. Its Spring spawning depends on the water temperature, usually beginning in the middle of May, but sometimes deferred to the middle of July. Spawning takes place in the evenings and early mornings at a water temperature of 18—21°C. The Catfish spawns in pairs the eggs being deposited into a previously prepared nest. After spawning the male guards the eggs until they have hatched. The number of eggs is considerable and depends on the weight of the fish, 10—13 thousand eggs representing 1 lb of its weight. In the earliest phase of development the young feed on plankton. At the end of the first year they become predatory, growing very quickly and attaining a weight of 5—6 lbs in their third year. The length of their life has not been accurately ascertained. A catfish of 180 lbs is 24 years old, so that a specimen weighing 500—650 lbs must be at least 80 years old.

In Europe the Catfish lives in the upper part of the Rhine and in the rivers east of the Rhine emptying into the Baltic, Black, Caspian or Aral Seas.

Where it is found it is of considerable industrial importance, if occurring in sufficient quantities. In carp ponds it represents an important supplementary predatory fish. It is also very much sought after by anglers.

(M.)

Silurus glanis

The European Eel

Anguilla anguilla (LINNAEUS, 1758)

Because of its complex life the Eel used to be considered the most mysterious fish. In European waters it is the only representative of the family *Anguillidae* comprising only one genus — *Anguilla* — with some 10 species.

The Eel has a typically snake-like body of circular cross-section in the anterior half, the posterior half being laterally compressed. Its vertebral column contains 110—119 vertebrae. The head is small and pointed. The female can be distinguished by having a wider head than the male. The body is covered with very small scales which do not overlap. The strong jaws are well provided with tapered teeth. The mouth is small and bordered with large lips, but can be opened into a considerable gape. The skin is thick and very slimy. The ventral fins are missing, a feature distinguishing the Eel from all other fishes. The gill slits are situated in the immediate vicinity of pectoral fins which contain 15—29 soft rays and are the only paired fins of the Eel. The anal fin has 176—249 soft rays, the caudal fin 7—12 soft rays. When descending the rivers to the sea the Eel becomes silvery.

The Eel avoids swiftly flowing waters, but otherwise occurs everywhere. It is nocturnal, spending the day in the mud, and leaving the bottom of the river at night to hunt for food. It feeds mostly on small animals, thus competing with other bottom-living fishes. It spawns in the Spring, in the so-called Sargasso Sea in the Caribbean. It spawns in the depths of the sea, dying immediately afterwards. The young eels — *Leptocephalus* — are entirely unlike the adult fish; they float passively in the Gulf Stream until the third year when they reach the European coast and ascend into fresh waters metamorphosing into elvers on the way. When sexually mature, they migrate down the rivers back to the sea.

The Eel occurs in all European waters accessible from the sea, from the river Pechora emptying into the Arctic Ocean to the Don emptying into the Azov Sea. In the Danube basin it is rather rare.

In the coastal countries where it occurs in abundant quantities it is of considerable industrial importance; its importance is also constantly rising in river fishery. Because of its valuable and tasty flesh it is also very popular with anglers. It can be successfully caught on rainworms or small fishes, such as Perch, Bleak, or Pope, using always heavy or medium tackle.

(M.)

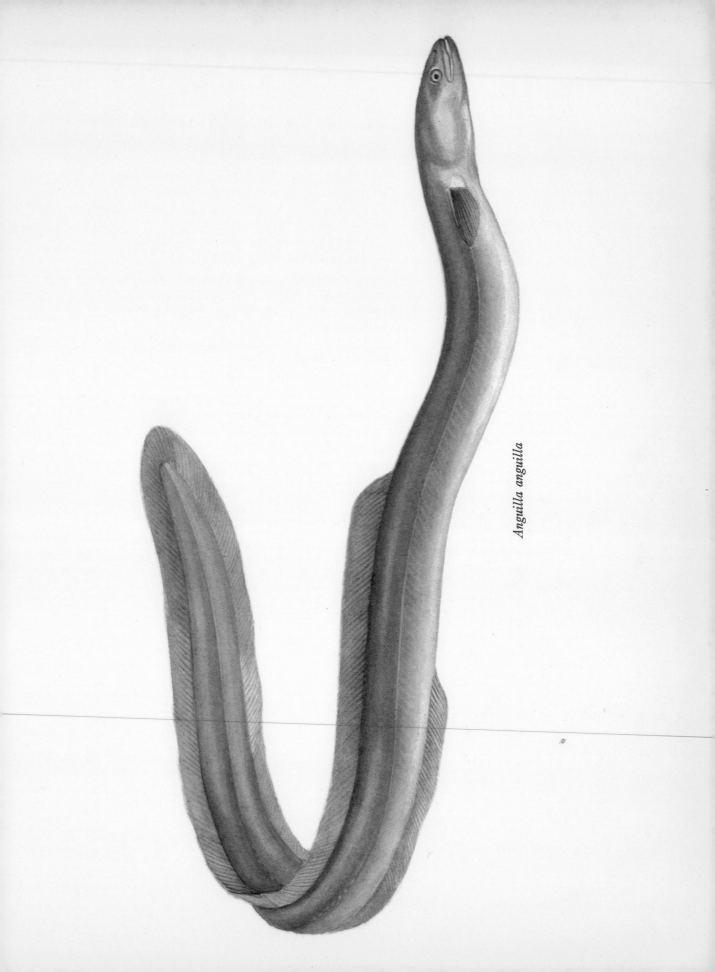

Anguilla anguilla

The Burbot

Lota lota (LINNAEUS, 1758)

This nocturnal fish of clean brooks, rivers and lakes is the only freshwater representative of the well-known and very widely spread marine Cod family — *Gadidae*.

The body of the Burbot is elongated, covered with small scales; its head has a typical, vertically compressed shape recalling the head of a frog. The wide mouth is provided with small teeth, the lower jaw terminating in a single barbel. The dorsal fin is divided into two parts, the anterior short, the posterior of considerable length reaching as far as the caudal fin. The anal fin is of similar shape and length. The ventral fins are anterior to the pectoral fins and are pointed. The anterior part of the dorsal fin has 1 hard and 9—15 soft rays, the posterior part 2 hard and 68—93 soft rays, the anal fin comprising 63—85 soft rays. Its basic colour is brown to green-brown with dark, almost black, hues, and characteristic pale marbling pattern and blotches. The belly is grey or greyish yellow.

The Burbot is a cold-loving fish, its chief feeding and spawning season being the winter — a feature in which it differs from all other continental freshwater fishes. Considerable rise of water temperature in Summer brings the Burbot into a state of numbness as if the fish hibernated in Summer. At the end of Autumn and the beginning of Winter the Burbot becomes active again, being most agile and most voracious when the water is covered with ice — i.e. from December to March. The spawning season is very long, usually lasting from the end of December to the end of February, when the water temperature is very near 0° Centigrade. The number of eggs is enormous; one female can lay as many as 3 million.

The Burbot can live to an age of 20 years, attaining a length of over $3\frac{1}{2}$ feet and a weight of 50 lbs (Onega Sea, USSR). It is a nocturnal predatory fish, rarely hunting for food during the day, and feeds exclusively on fishes.

The habitat of the Burbot includes the rivers, lakes and bays of northern Europe and Asia as far as the 45th parallel to the South, sometimes exceeding this boundary and spreading even further south (in Europe the rivers Rhône, Seine, Loire, Danube and the lower reaches of the Kura). It occurs most frequently in the northern and eastern parts of the above area, the numbers diminishing towards the south and west. In England it occurs very rarely, being entirely absent from Scotland and Ireland.

In the territories where it abounds the Burbot is of considerable economic importance. It is caught in nets and on the hook and is highly appreciated for its tasty flesh and particularly for the large quantity of medically valuable oil extracted from its liver which accounts for 6—10 % of the overall body weight. In trout streams, however, the Burbot is undesirable. It is popular with anglers, though. When caught on the hook it offers sport similar to that of the Eel.

(H.)

Lota lota

The Large-mouthed Black Bass

Micropterus salmoides (LACÉPÈDE, 1802)

The Large-mouthed Black Bass is a domesticated species imported from America. It belongs to the family *Centrarchidae* whose members have a considerably protracted lower jaw and a wide mouth and are exclusively predatory fishes.

The Black Bass differs from the rest of the family in its longer body, arched back and large caudal fin. Its dorsal fins are also characteristic: the anterior has strong, short spines with 9 or 10 hard rays connected by a narrow membrane, the posterior is relatively higher, rounded, connected with the anterior, and reinforced with 12 or 13 soft rays. The long head occupies almost one third of the body length and terminates in a pointed mouth well equipped with small teeth. The lower jaw considerably exceeds the upper in length. The caudal fin is truncated and has 18 soft rays, the anal fin is long, rounded and has 3 hard and 10—12 soft rays. Both fins are fan-shaped. Hard, distinct scales cover the gill-covers. On the flanks the Black Bass has 62—68 transverse rows of scales, thus resembling its American relative, *Micropterus dolomieu* Lacépède, which has 72—85 rows of scales.

The habitat of the Black Bass is lakes and the lower reaches of slowly flowing rivers, in which it is found at the bottom. In the Spring it rises and moves to shallow waters for spawning which takes place in May and June. One female lays as many as 15 thousand very sticky eggs into a previously prepared place in the soft river or lake bottom; the male then guards the eggs and does not leave its progeny even after they have hatched. The young feed on plankton and small crustaceans, and later on small fishes.

The growth of the Black Bass is very variable. In its native country it reaches a weight of 9 lbs provided the feeding conditions are good, and may weigh as much as 17 lbs in the southern states of America. In European waters it grows to a weight of 1—2 lbs at the most.

In North America it is appreciated for its tasty flesh and relatively good growth both from the economic and from the angling points of view.

(M.)

Micropterus salmoides

The Pumpkinseed Sunfish

Lepomis gibbosus (LINNAEUS, 1758)

The Pumpkinseed Sunfish is very varied in colouring and reaches a length of 6—8 inches in its native country. It has a short, high, compressed body with a large, blunt head, red eyes, and a wide mouth provided with small teeth. The anterior dorsal fin is low, spiny, and short, the posterior continuing the former is higher, longer and provided with 10—12 soft rays. The anal fin has 1 hard and 5 soft rays, the pectoral fins being short, containing 11—14 soft rays each. Ctenoid scales cover the whole body.

The Sunfish inhabits deep, still waters. It spawns in May and June in sandy places, the male guarding the eggs until they have hatched. Growth is slow; in European waters the fish grows to a length of up to 6 ins. It feeds on small aquatic fauna and fishes.

The native country of the Sunfish is North America; it was imported to Europe at the end of last century. Because of its small size and voracity (particularly of eggs and young fish) it is undesirable in open waters, and its further spread should be controlled.

(M.)

The Brown Bullhead

Ictalurus nebulosus (LE SUEUR, 1819)

The Brown Bullhead was imported to Europe from North America as the only representative of the family *Ictaluridae*.

A characteristic feature is two pairs of barbels on its upper jaw, the pair growing at the corners of its mouth being longer than the other pair growing in the vicinity of its nostrils. On the lower jaw there are two more pairs of barbels. The mouth is provided with small teeth, the body is devoid of scales and has a very slimy skin. The dorsal fin has one hard and 6 soft rays, the adipose fin being without rays. The pectoral fins have one hard and 8 soft rays. The anal fin is long and comprises 19—24 soft rays, and the wide, forked caudal fin has 19 soft rays.

In Europe the Brown Bullhead has been domesticated particularly in slow-running waters. It spawns in May and June in pairs like the Catfish. The female lays 3—4 thousand eggs 3—4 mm in diameter into a previously prepared pit in the sand, the male guarding the eggs until they have hatched and even leading the shoal of young for a short while. It does not grow as large as the Catfish, reaching a length of only 16 ins and a weight of 4 lbs in its native country, and much less in Europe. It is very voracious and feeds on small animals as well as the benthos.

The original habitat of the Brown Bullhead is North America. In Europe it is of no economic importance.

(M.)

Lepomis gibbosus

Ictalurus nebulosus

The Pike-Perch

Stizostedion lucioperca (LINNAEUS, 1758)

After the Pike the Pike-Perch is the most popular and most widely spread predatory fish of notable economic importance, including the related Eastern Pike-Perch, *Stizostedion volgense* (Gmelin, 1788). The Pike Perches living in European waters are closely related to the American Perches.

The body is symmetrical, the head narrow with a large mouth, and the coloration variegated. The flanks bear 8—12 characteristic brownish-black bands which are particularly marked in the young. In older specimens the bands break up into separate irregular blotches. Black spots are also found between the spines of the anterior dorsal fin arranged in ten irregular rows, and between the rays of the posterior dorsal fin. In the spawning season the belly of the male is marbled blue, that of the female pure white. The two dorsal fins are separated by a small gap. The anterior dorsal fin has 13—17 hard spines, the posterior having 1—3 hard and 19—27 soft rays. The lateral line comprises 80—97 scales. The mouth is provided with numerous small and several bigger tapered teeth.

The Pike-Perch lives in deep water with sandy or gravelly bottom. It is exacting with respect to the oxygen content of the water. It is a crepuscular fish, leaving its shelter in the evening to hunt for food, frequenting even shallow places and hunting even if the water has grown cold. It spawns in April and March in pairs. The female lays 100—300 thousand eggs 1.5 mm in diameter on sand or weed roots previously prepared for this purpose. The male guards the eggs while they are hatching. The young hatch in 10—15 days, at a water temperature of 12—14°C. In their third year the young grow to a length of 12—20 ins and a weight of 1—3 lbs, the maximum attainable size is 25—30 lbs at $3\frac{1}{2}$—$4\frac{1}{2}$ ft. The young begin by feeding on plankton, later becoming predatory and feeding on small fishes.

The Pike-Perch came to Central Europe from the East soon after the end of the Ice Age, the western boundary of its natural habitat being represented by the Elbe and the Danube. It also lives in the rivers emptying into the Baltic and Black Seas as well as the Caspian and the Aral Seas, and in the river Maritsa.

The Pike-Perch is one of the most valuable predatory fishes of the lower parts of rivers and is very much sought after by anglers. As a rule it is caught by hand fishing without float or by spinning, using a live or a dead fish as bait. A struggle with a large Pike-Perch in the evening is an exciting and unforgettable experience.

(M.)

Stizostedion lucioperca

The Eastern Pike-Perch

Stizostedion volgense (GMELIN, 1788)

The Eastern Pike-Perch is very similar to its relative, the European Pike-Perch. It lives in the rivers emptying into the Black and Caspian Seas.

The Eastern Pike-Perch differs from its European relative in the general structure of its body, older specimens being higher. There is also a basic difference in the numbers of fin rays. The Eastern Pike-Perch has 2 hard and 9 or 10 soft rays in the anal fin, 12—16 hard rays in the anterior dorsal fin and 1 or 2 hard and 20—22 soft rays in the posterior dorsal fin. The lateral line comprises 70—83 scales. In contrast to those of the European Pike-Perch the front teeth of the Eastern Pike-Perch are not longer than the others.

There are no major differences in mode of life between the two species. The Eastern Pike-Perch favours deep, sandy places with abundant shelter. It spawns from the beginning to the end of May; low water temperature, however, can considerably delay spawning. The males attain sexual maturity when 8—12 ins long, the females usually later. After the Spring thaw they descend as far as the estuaries, ascending back into the rivers in the autumn and hibernating there in the deepest places all through the winter. The Eastern Pike-Perch is less voracious than the European variety, feeding also on small crustaceans, although its staple diet consists of small fishes. It grows to a length of 18 ins and a weight of $2-2\frac{1}{2}$ lbs, rarely reaching 22 ins and 4—6 lbs.

The Eastern Pike-Perch occurs in eastern Europe, in the Volga, the Don, the Dnieper and the Dniester, and rarely in the Tisa and Morava. In Central Europe it is rather rare.

In East European rivers it represents an economically important fish. Anglers catch it by similar methods to those used for the Perch, either on dead fish or a strip of meat. Its flesh is most valuable at the end of August.

(M.)

Stizostedion volgense

The Perch

Perca fluviatilis LINNAEUS, 1758

The Perch represents the very old family *Percidae* which embraces 15 genera and about 96 species living in the waters of North America, Europe, and western and northern Asia. Characteristic features of this family are the ventral fins situated below the pectoral fins, two closely linked dorsal fins, and the number of hard rays in the dorsal fins.

The Perch has a rather high, slightly compressed body and a tapered head with a very large central mouth provided with uniform dentition. The large eyes are mobile. The characteristic feature of the anterior dorsal fin is the vivid black spot at the end in the middle of the back. The anterior dorsal fin has 13—17 hard spines, the posterior dorsal fin is higher and has 1 or 2 hard and 13—15 soft rays. The ventral fins are placed forward below the pectoral fins which have 2 hard and 8 or 9 soft rays. The scales cover not only the body but also the face and the gill covers. The lateral line comprises 62—74 scales, with 7—10 rows above and 12—18 rows of scales below it.

The Perch is a gregarious fish living in shoals in fresh, salt, and brackish waters, avoiding cold, swiftly flowing waters. If it penetrates into the latter, it never breeds.

Spawning takes place in April and May; the female lays the eggs in long ribbons on stones, submerged branches, hanging roots, etc. The number of eggs produced depends on the size of the specimen and can vary between 20 and 200 thousand. The growth of the young depends on the size of the reservoir or stream and the quantity of food available. If food is scarce, the Perch attains an average length of 6—10 ins, if food is abundant it grows to a weight of 4—5 lbs, rarely up to 8 lbs. The Perch is very voracious and devours everything living from eggs to fishes.

Apart from Scotland, the South-East peninsulas and Norway, its range includes the whole of Europe and Asia and the rivers emptying into the Arctic Ocean.

In closed reservoirs where it is abundant and remains rather small it is considered undesirable. It has excellent flesh, however, and large specimens are very much sought after. In rivers it is valuable both from the economic and angling points of view.

(M.)

Perca fluviatilis

The Zingel

Zingel zingel (LINNAEUS, 1758)

The interesting fishes of the genus *Zingel* differ from the other members of the family *Percidae* in their ventral mouth, narrow, spindle-shaped body, and scales covering the gill covers. The mouth is provided with small teeth fixed to both maxillaries.

The eyes are particularly attractive, they have a green sheen in the dark, are mobile and can turn in different directions to observe the surroundings.

The anterior dorsal fin has 13—15 hard spines, the posterior dorsal fin one hard and 18—21 soft rays, the anal fin one hard and 11—13 soft rays, the ventral fin one hard and 5 soft rays, and the pectoral fins have 14 soft rays each. The lateral line comprises 83—95 scales.

The fish lives in shallow, clean, swiftly flowing rivers. It has mostly nocturnal habits, leaving its shelter in the evening to hunt for food. It lives at the bottom, feeding on larvae, worms, molluscs and crustaceans. It spawns in the Spring (May) in running water with a stony bottom, laying its eggs on the stones. On an average it attains a length of 10—14 ins, rarely 16—18 ins, and a weight of 2 lbs.

It is found in the Danube and its tributaries, the Prut and Dniester.

(M.)

The Streber

Zingel streber (SIEBOLD, 1863)

Similar to *Zingel zingel*, but still more slender. The species differ from one another in the number of rays in the dorsal fin, *Zingel streber* having 8 or 9 rays in the anterior dorsal fin, its anal fin having one hard and 10—12 soft rays. The lateral line comprises 70—82 scales.

In the mode of life *Zingel streber* does not differ much from its relative. It usually lives in deep pools below the stream which it leaves in the evening — or, when it rains, even during the day — to hunt for food. It spawns in March, the female laying eggs 2 mm in diameter on the stony bottom of running water. The fish grows slowly reaching a maximum length of 4—6 ins and a weight of 2—3½ ozs.

Zingel streber lives in the Danube basin and in the rivers Prut and Vardar emptying into the Aegean Sea.

With its small size and relatively rare occurrence, it is of no economic or angling importance.

(M.)

Zingel zingel

Zingel streber

The Pope

Acerina cernua (LINNAEUS, 1758)

The Pope differs from all other genera of the *Percidae* in the number of the rays in its anal fin, less than in the Perch and Pike-Perch, and by the absence of scales from its head.

The body of the Pope is more elongated than that of the Perch, the ventral line is straight, and the head is blunt. The eyes are large and distinct. The dorsal fins are combined into one containing 11—16 hard and 11—15 soft rays. The anal fin has 2 hard and 5 or 6 soft rays. The lateral line comprises 35—40 scales.

The Pope inhabits deep, slow-running water with a sandy bottom. During the day it stays at the bottom, leaving its shelter in the evening to hunt for food in more shallow places. It spawns at the end of April and in May, the number of eggs laid being about 100 thousand. The young hatch after 9—14 days. The Pope feeds on small animals, particularly the eggs of other fishes. It grows to a maximum length of 12 ins.

Its range covers northern and Central Europe, extending to the west into north-eastern France and the whole of eastern Europe, the rivers emptying into the Arctic Ocean, the Danube basin, and the tributaries of the Caspian and Aral Seas. In the regions where it is abundant it is of industrial importance, and represents an important food of the Pike-Perch.

(M.)

The Schrätzer

Acerina schraetzer (LINNAEUS, 1758)

The Schrätzer is slenderer than the Pope, has a long, pointed head, the lower line of the head and of the belly being almost straight. The body narrows towards the caudal fin, the anterior dorsal fin being longer than the posterior which, on the other hand, has considerably longer rays. The Schrätzer differs from the Pope in the rays in its dorsal fin which number 17—19 hard and 12—14 soft rays. The anal fin has 2 hard and 6 or 7 soft rays, the ventral fins having one hard and 5 soft rays each.

The Schrätzer inhabits deep pools with a sandy bottom. The fish is exacting with regard to the oxygen content of the water. It spawns in March and April in shoals; the female lays between 6 and 8 thousand eggs, 0.9 mm in diameter.

In size the Schrätzer does not differ much from the Pope, attaining a length of 12 ins. It feeds mainly on worms, larvae, and crustaceans, also favouring the eggs of other fishes.

It lives only in the Danube basin and in the river Kamchia in Bulgaria.

Because of its small size and rare occurrence it is of no economic importance. (M.)

Acerina cernua

Acerina schraetzer

The Three-Spined Stickleback

Gasterosteus aculeatus (LINNAEUS, 1758)

This small fish of the family *Gasterosteidae* is particularly interesting to aquarists.

It has a slender, spindle-shaped, compressed body with a relatively large head and a protrusible mouth provided with fine small teeth. The flanks of the Stickleback are covered with irregularly arranged bony shields. Another characteristic feature is the dorsal fin with 3 hard and 10—12 soft rays. In front of it there are three spines, the second of which is longest and the third very small.

The Stickleback is a non-exacting fish living near the banks of large rivers. It spawns in April and June. Prior to spawning the male finds a place among the weeds and builds a globular nest into which the female deposits the eggs. The food of the Stickleback consists of zooplankton. It occurs along the European coast from Novaya Zemlya as far as the north-western coast of the Black Sea, the coast of Iceland, Greenland and New York as well as the Pacific coast.

(M.)

Miller's Thumb (Bullhead)

Cottus poecilopus (HECKEL, 1836)
Cottus gobio (LINNAEUS, 1758)

The Bullheads — ghoulish-looking inhabitants of clean mountain brooks and spates — are members of the large family *Cottidae* which includes mostly marine fishes and only a few freshwater species. Their ventral fins are shifted forward, being situated right under the pectoral fins.

The low, spindle-shaped body of the Bullhead is well adapted to life at the bottom of very swift brooks and below boulders. The head is very large, compressed from above, its appearance recalling that of a frog. The mouth is large and well stocked with small teeth. The dorsal fin has 6—9 hard and 15—19 soft rays, and the anal fin has 10—14 soft rays.

The Bullheads are characteristic inhabitants of mountain rivers and brooks with a high oxygen content. They live separately, usually concealed under boulders. In the spawning season the female sticks the eggs on the bottom of stones. The eggs form a yellowish pile which the male very carefully guards and protects. Both species attain a length of 4 ins, exceptionally 6—8 ins.

Distribution: *Cottus poecilopus* lives in the rivers emptying into the Baltic Sea, in the basins of the Danube and the Dniester as well as in the Far East, in the basins of the rivers Amur and Sungari. *Cottus gobio* is even more widely spread, its habitat covering the whole of Europe from northern Spain as far as the Ural Mountains. It is not found in the Caucasus, South Italy, Greece, Scotland, Ireland, Jutland or Norway.

Both species are of importance only in waters of intensive trout rearing, where they are considered to be highly undesirable.

(M.)

Gasterosteus aculeatus

Cottus poecilopus

Cottus gobio

INDEX OF LATIN NAMES

INDEX OF COMMON NAMES